A Popular Guide to
CHINESE
VEGETABLES

A Popular Guide to
CHINESE VEGETABLES

Martha Dahlen
Karen Phillipps

CROWN PUBLISHERS, INC.
NEW YORK

First published in the United States of America by Crown Publishers, Inc., One Park Avenue, New York, New York 10016 and published simultaneously in Canada by General Publishing Company Limited.

Library of Congress Cataloging in Publication Data

Dahlen, Martha.
    Popular Guide to Chinese Vegetables.

    "Originally written and published in Hong Kong as two volumes entitled A Guide to Chinese Market Vegetables and A Further Guide to Chinese Market Vegetables"—Foreword.
    Includes Index.
    1. Cookery (Vegetables) 2. Cookery, Chinese.
I. Phillipps, Karen. II. Title.
TX801.D24 1983   641.6'5'095127   83-1876

ISBN 0-517-55054-7 (paper)

First published in Hong Kong in 1983
by South China Morning Post Ltd., Publications Division,
Tong Chong Street, Quarry Bay,
Hong Kong

Printed in Hong Kong by Yee Tin Tong Printing Press Ltd.,
Tong Chong Street, Quarry Bay, Hong Kong

10 9 8 7 6 5 4 3 2 1

First American Edition

TABLE OF CONTENTS

FOREWORD

...PAST

This book was originally written and published in Hong Kong as two volumes entitled *A Guide to Chinese Market Vegetables* and *A Further Guide to Chinese Market Vegetables*. Although written specifically for non-Chinese shoppers in the intimidating maze of Hong Kong's street markets, the books met such an enthusiastic reception elsewhere that this consolidated edition is now in your hands.

...PRESENT

The following pages present practical descriptions of Chinese vegetables and an introduction to modern, home-style Cantonese cooking. For the experimental cook and vegetable gourmet, Oriental markets are treasure troves. The seasonal variety of greens, melons, roots and fruits as well as the perennial variety of dried, canned and preserved foods amazes the eye, teases the palate and leaves the mind bewildered. "It must be edible, but what is it and how do I cook it?" Here you will find illustrations of more than 70 different Chinese vegetables plus our attempts to answer these questions clearly, concisely and usefully. As this is first and foremost a book about (non-racist!) vegetables, we also include suggestions as to how to prepare these vegetables in Western style.

The second, and secondary, purpose of this book is to introduce ordinary Cantonese cooking. With the instructions and recipes included here you will hopefully discover, as we have, that home cooking is both easier and more delicious than restaurant fare. Universally, it seems, good cooking is a matter of sound ingredients and sound technique. Royal chefs may prepare elaborate dishes from exotic ingredients, but the essence of quality is still the small scale, experienced technique and fresh ingredients with which they work.

The cooking advice presented in this book comes from modern Cantonese home-makers and cooks. It was learned while eating with families, watching amahs and mothers cook, and listening to the advice of friends and vegetable vendors. Consequently, our "recipes" are simple, general guidelines rather than elaborate formulae; they require only a couple of versatile pots rather than an arsenal of equipment; and seasoning can be as simple as salt—although elaboration according to taste and means is certainly possible as well.

Because we present modern Cantonese cookery, you will find in this book, as we find in Hong Kong markets, recently-introduced Western vegetables side by side with ancient and traditional Chinese ones. Both can become "authentic" Chinese dishes, because the essence of Chinese cuisine lies in the intent and ability to produce appetizing, flavourful and nutritious food, no matter what the ingredients.

...FUTURE

Armed with the illustrations and information here, anyone should be able to identify, select, prepare and cook these vegetables with confidence—and with Cantonese flavour. Familiarity may breed contempt, but in this case we hope it becomes a bridge between ignorance and bliss for those who enjoy good food.

APOLOGIES

We warn you that trying to match our Romanized names of the vegetables, sauces and drygoods with names on bottles in stores will be frustrating. The Romanized spellings given here represent Cantonese pronunciation according to the system of Herklots (see Appendix). Meanwhile, names on bottles may be written according to another system of Romanization or another Chinese dialect, or may be another name altogether. In any case, rendering a two-dimensional (i.e., tonal) language like Chinese with a one-dimensional alphabet like the Roman will always be artificial and approximate. Thus, when words are necessary, we suggest that you match pronunciations not spellings (e.g., "baak choi" sounds like "bok choy;" "dau see" sounds similar to "dou shih"); or that you match the Chinese characters.

Finally we must emphasize that we are not authorities on Chinese food or cuisine. We are simply great admirers of Cantonese home-style cooking, seeking to share our knowledge and admiration. Certainly our view is limited. Not every Chinese cooks as we describe, just as not all vegetables will match our illustrations. Nevertheless, in both cases some do, and, for the cooks, to what extent the "some" represents a majority is not as important as the fact that their advice is deliciously sound.

CHINESE COOKING UTENSILS

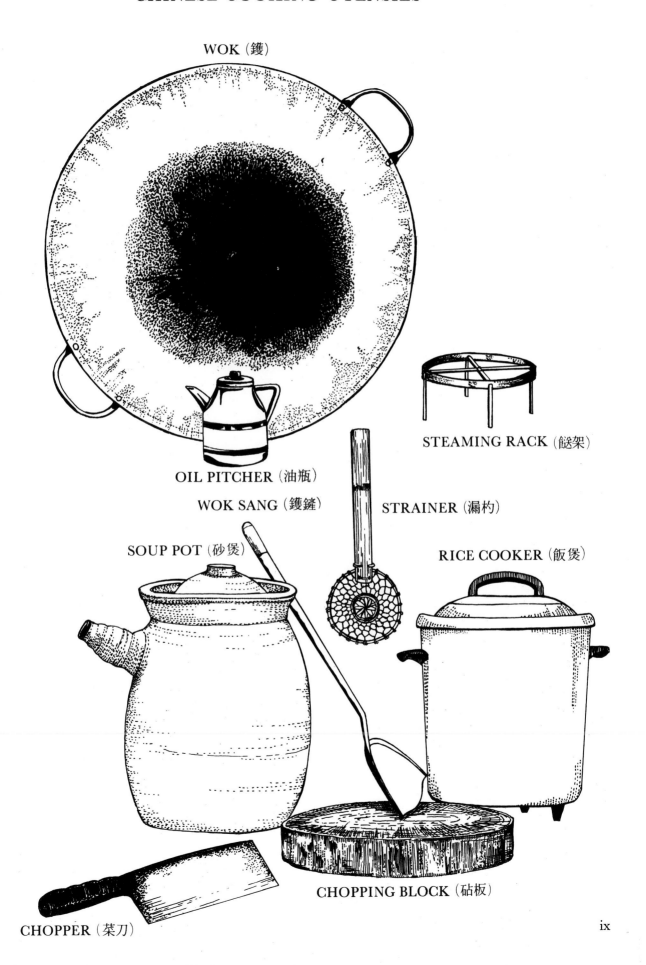

WOK (鑊)

OIL PITCHER (油瓶)

STEAMING RACK (餸架)

WOK SANG (鑊鏟)

STRAINER (漏杓)

SOUP POT (砂煲)

RICE COOKER (飯煲)

CHOPPING BLOCK (砧板)

CHOPPER (菜刀)

ACKNOWLEDGEMENTS

We wish to express hearty and sincere appreciation to all our Chinese friends who have patiently and generously shared their cooking experience with us. Mr. Lam Wai-sing and Mrs. Nancy Chan deserve special thanks.

BASIC CHINESE COOKING

STAPLE INGREDIENTS

Rice. Good rice, properly cooked, is the *sine qua non* of a Cantonese meal. For this purpose, white rice is preferred to brown or red, and long-grain is preferred to short-grain. (The latter sorts of rice are used to make rice porridge, known as congee or "jook" 粥, one variation of which is described on p. 39). Cooked rice grains should be whole, separate, tender and sweet. Many varieties exist which seem to differ mainly according to country of cultivation. The fragrant rice from Thailand ("heung mai" 香米) is one of the choicest.

Oil. Choice of oil subtly influences the flavour of dishes, but convenience and availability seem to determine the choice among Asian cooks. Malaysians use coconut oil; Indians use mustard oil; mainland Chinese use a sort of mustard oil; many northern Chinese use much sesame oil; while Hong Kong Chinese use peanut oil, corn oil or lard. Of the vegetable oils, peanut oil is particularly complimentary to and compatible with Cantonese cooking. Heating it to just below the smoking point improves its flavour, so when using peanut oil be sure to heed directions specifying "cooked oil."

METHODS

Cooking Rice. Undoubtedly the greatest—and possibly the only revolutionary—gift modern science has given to Chinese home cuisine is the electric rice cooker. Cookers range in size from two-man, six-bowl capacity, to the restaurant size capable of cooking rice for thirty people. They can not only cook rice, but also boil soup, boil congee, and steam dishes of meat and vegetables (thus rendering other pots unnecessary) in a kitchen, office, dorm or shop.

As illustrated, a rice cooker looks and functions essentially like a crock-pot. It consists of a removable aluminium pan which holds rice and water, and the pot body which contains a heating element with thermostat inside and a lighted on-off button outside. To use it, place the desired quantity of raw rice in the aluminium pan, rinse it three times to remove excess starch, and then add cooking water. Measure water either by volume (equal quantities rice and water for Chinese white rice) or by hand (when the fingertips rest lightly on the submerged surface of the raw rice, the water level should reach halfway between the first and second knuckle of the middle finger). Dry the outside of the aluminium pan, set it in the cooker body, replace the lid, and depress the "cook" button. The light inside the button will immediately begin to glow, indicating the heating element is on. When the rice is cooked (i.e., when the temperature of the pan rises above the boiling point of water because all water has been absorbed by the rice or steamed away), the button pops up and the light goes out.

To cook rice in a saucepan, use slightly more water than specified above, bring to a boil, reduce heat to *very low* and allow it to simmer gently until rice is cooked, 20–30 minutes later. With a heavy iron, or enamelled iron, pan and an electric burner, bring the rice to a boil, cover, turn off the burner and wait 20 minutes. The pot and burner should retain enough heat to cook the rice. After 20 minutes check, then reheat gently to finish the cooking and to serve.

Seasoning raw meat. Chop chicken into bite-size pieces, preferably strips; cut beef or pork across the grain into thin strips. Mix the meat with salt, sugar, cornstarch, cooked oil and light soy sauce, using $\frac{1}{4}-\frac{1}{2}$ teaspoon each for about $\frac{1}{2}$ cup shredded meat according to taste.

This seasoning procedure is fairly universal and is done anywhere from ten minutes to an hour or more before cooking. In the recipes that follow, "meat, seasoned" means to prepare it as described above.

1

Seasoning fresh fish, shrimp or prawns, and liver. Fresh whole fish should be scaled, cleaned, rinsed with water and rubbed lightly with salt. Shrimp, cleaned or whole, should be rinsed to clean and tossed with salt to remove slime and to firm the flesh. Juice of freshly grated ginger or shreds of fresh ginger soaked in wine is reputed to kill off flavours of less-than-fresh fish and liver. Thus, use either of the above as a marinade for shredded liver, chopped fish and shrimp—particularly frozen ones—before cooking. White pepper added during cooking will also help mask undesirable tastes.

Stir-frying. The principle of stir-frying is first to seal savoury juices inside the food by quickly, lightly coating it with hot oil, and then to cook each oil-sealed piece with intense steam. The method is this:

Heat the wok. Add oil according to how much food you will cook; experience and taste will teach you proportions. When the oil is quite hot—denoted by smoke at the edges—gently splash it up the wok's sides with the wok-sang in order to coat all surfaces which food will hit.

At this point most Cantonese cooks will add a crushed clove of garlic (and a crushed slice of fresh ginger for certain foods), cook it momentarily until fragrant, and then discard.

Add the washed, drained, chopped vegetables all at once. A loud, continuous hiss should result. The Cantonese call this "wok hay" 鑊氣 and believe its quality (i.e., volume and duration) is directly proportional to the quality of the finished dish. As soon as you have added pieces of food to the wok, begin tossing them with the wok-sang in order to coat them quickly and evenly with oil. When they begin to cook, becoming fragrant, wilted and bright in colour, sprinkle with salt. Leafy vegetables will be done after another minute or two of tossing. For more solid vegetables, add a little water to create steam, and clamp the lid on. When you judge the vegetables are done, remove the lid, toss them and correct seasoning with soy sauce or salt. The vegetables taste and look better if you lift the lid only once, when they are done, and if there is very little liquid remaining.

In a mixture, add slow-cooking ingredients first, faster cooking ones later, or stir-fry them separately. With mixed meat and vegetables, always stir-fry separately and combine at the end to blend flavours. The Cantonese unequivocally recommend frying the meat first, presumably because meat takes longer to cook and survives waiting in better condition than vegetables. In this case, scrub the hot wok quickly with water and a brush between meat and veg.

Proper stir-frying depends on having a heat source strong enough to maintain "wok hay" throughout the cooking process. Woks are recommended for this because their concave design distributes the heat over a large surface area, accommodates large and small volumes of food equally well, withstands sudden changes of temperature, and encourages quick evaporation of unwanted water. The best ones are made of steel and seasoned black.

Despite its attributes, a wok may not be the best—nor is it the only—way to produce "wok hay." A gas burner with a fitting to support a wok is the best arrangement. On electric burners, metal collars are sold to support the wok but by raising the wok above the heat they effectively prevent it from ever becoming hot enough. In such a case, a cast-iron skillet with tall sides or a sturdy saucepan may be the best answer. In any case, note that stir-frying is not the only method of cooking Chinese food so that if stir-frying is difficult in your kitchen, try more braised, steamed or deep-fried dishes.

Deep-frying. The critical factor here is temperature. The oil must be hot enough to cook the ingredients quickly without soaking them in oil, but not hot enough to burn the outside before the inside is cooked. The quantity of oil must be enough that adding food does not drop its temperature below the critical oil-soaking temperature.

In practice this means: (1) Use at least four times as much by volume of oil as ingredients to be fried at one time. (2) Heat it to the appropriate temperature. Chinese cooks use a bamboo chopstick as a thermometer. When a bamboo chopstick inserted in the middle of the oil causes bubbles to rise around it, the oil is ready. (3) Foods to be fried should be cut in uniform, small or thin pieces, kept dry, and added in small quantities.

Steaming. This technique is used particularly for fresh fish, savoury egg custards, rice flour puddings and minced meat mixtures. Accomplish it as follows:

Place a steaming rack in a pot. The rack may be a purchased one as illustrated, anything comparable you can fashion from sturdy wire, or a brick; in a wok you may also use a grid or a pair of sticks wedged in about $\frac{1}{3}$ of the way up the wok's sides. Fill the pot with 1–2 inches of water, cover and bring to a boil. When the water reaches a rolling boil, place the dish of prepared food on the rack, recover the pot, and maintain the water at a gentle boil until the food is cooked. Alternatively—and more commonly among Cantonese—the rack is set in the rice cooker so that the dish cooks in the steam of the cooking rice.

Shallow round enamelled metal pans are the most convenient dishes to use for steaming food because they are unbreakable and conduct heat quickly. In Hong Kong most Cantonese households have a nested series of such pans varying in diameter from 3–8″—and most have a rice cooker twice as big as necessary in order to have room above the rice for steaming dishes.

In restaurants, steaming is done with bamboo steamers over woks of boiling water. The steamers come in sections, each section consisting of a circumference of bamboo and a grid inside to support the food. The sections fit on top of each other, with a lid to terminate the stack. Bamboo is better than metal as a steaming container because it absorbs and leaks water rather than causing it to condense and drip onto the food.

Creating Cantonese Gravy. To thicken a sauce or to make Cantonese "heen," combine cornstarch with 2–3 parts cold water, mix to homogeneity, add to the food while stirring, and cook for a minute or two until it thickens. Generally 2 teaspoons of cornstarch will thicken 1 cup of liquid to a medium consistency.

Traditional Cantonese cooks prefer to use a bean flour, "dau fun" 豆粉, rather than cornstarch because the former thickens faster and seems to hold its thickness longer.

SEASONING SUNDRIES

The following dried and preserved foods and sauces are both common—meaning they should be readily available—and versatile—meaning they will enable you to create a variety of tastes at any single meal with whatever meats, fish and vegetables are available.

All dried foods should keep indefinitely if stored very dry, in tightly-lidded containers, preferably out of the sun.

Light Soy Sauce (豉油) See yau; (生抽) Sang chau. This is the best grade of soy sauce. "Light" means it is not thick or viscous, and has a delicate, fine flavour. Use this for final seasoning of soups, stir-fried and steamed dishes, and as a table sauce.

Dark Soy Sauce (老抽) Lo chau. "Dark" here means thick and of stronger flavour. There are a number of types, each of which has been fermented with a different variety of ingredients, such as mushrooms, ginger, etc., and all of which stain food black. Lo chau is particularly used to give rich flavour and dark colour to braised or long-cooked dishes and sauces.

Fermented Black Beans. (豆豉) Dau see. These are whole soybeans which have been cooked, salted and fermented. They are black in colour, rather soft in texture, with each bean separate and measuring about $\frac{1}{4}$″ in length.

These beans are one of the most versatile, convenient, economical and flavourful Oriental seasonings. The Cantonese usually mash them with garlic and stir-fry or braise them with pork, beef, shellfish, fish or vegetables, particularly with green and red peppers for colour.

General directions for making **black bean sauce** are as follows:

Use approximately twice as much, by volume, of black beans as garlic. Crush the garlic cloves by smashing them with a single blow of a heavy object (flat side of a cleaver) on a cutting board. Remove the papery husk, then put both beans and garlic in a small bowl and mash together, either with a spoon or the butt of the cleaver's handle. Approximately 1 tablespoon of mash will season 1–2 cups of food.

3

To cook, add the mash to the hot oil before the ingredients. In a mixture, add the mash just before the last batch of ingredients to be fried, return all the rest to the wok, season with a pinch of sugar and light soy sauce, and, if desired, add some water with cornstarch to create a sauce.

Vary the sauce from heavy to light. For dark, thick, rich sauce, especially for braised dishes, use more beans and garlic, thoroughly pulverise them, and season the sauce with both dark and light soy sauces. Cover and simmer briefly to develop full flavour. For lighter, more delicate sauces, as for fish or chicken, use less and mash less vigorously in order to leave most of the beans whole.

In the recipes to come, whenever "black bean sauce" is specified, refer to the directions above.

Winter Mushrooms (冬菇) Dong gwoo. Known as "shiitake" to the Japanese and *Lentinus edodes* to the botanists, these mushrooms have been cultivated in the southern temperate parts of Asia for more than 1,000 years. In Japan they are cooked fresh; in China they are always dried and then reconstituted; in both countries they are expensive but highly esteemed for their distinct, robust flavour and succulent texture. Cantonese cooks use dong gwoo both as a seasoning, minced in small quantities, and as a vegetable, whole or sliced, in boiled, braised, steamed and stir-fry combinations.

The best winter mushrooms have thick caps, 1–2″ in diameter, light brown in colour, with prominent white cracks and a savoury fragrance. Serve these whole. Use cheaper, larger, darker ones for boiling in soup or stir-frying in slices. In any case, buy only those which are quite dry, lack signs of insect damage, particularly on the underside of the cap, and have a good fragrance.

To use, remove tough stems and save for soup. Soak caps in water at room temperature for at least 15 minutes. Drain, saving soaking water for later cooking, and squeeze.

Dried Shrimp (蝦米) Ha maai. The larger in size and darker pink in colour, the better the quality and higher the price. Some people nibble them straight as a snack. Cantonese cooks soak them in water at room temperature 15 minutes or more, pick over to remove all remnants of shells and legs, then use in cooking.

Ha maai are used in small quantities as a seasoning, not as a substitute for fresh shrimp. They are minced with pork and winter mushrooms in fillings or stuffings of various sorts, or fried with ginger in oil before stir-frying or boiling soup. Generally, they are considered to be compatible with cabbages, beans and bean curds of all sorts.

4

Mungbean Vermicelli (粉絲) Fun see. These are thread-like translucent noodles made from the starch of mungbeans. The confusion of strands is folded into and sold as neat rectangular bunches 4–5″ long or in plastic packages. Mungbean vermicelli has little taste and is used primarily to thicken sauce or soup.

To use, soak strands in water at room temperature 15 minutes or more. Cut with kitchen scissors or a small knife into shorter, more manageable lengths. Alternatively, the dried strands may be deep-fried and served crisp under a sauce of stir-fried meat and vegetables.

Oyster Sauce (蠔油) Ho yau. This is a richly flavoured, slightly sweet sauce prepared from, coincidentally enough, oysters. Tastes of different brands vary considerably; price is usually a reliable barometer of quality.

This is principally used to season boiled vegetables and to flavour braised vegetarian dishes.

Jew's Ear Mushrooms (云耳) Wan yee. Both Chinese and English names of this mushroom derive from the fact that the fresh ones have a convoluted shape and thin, smooth texture reminiscent of a human ear. Dried wan yee look like crumpled bits of dark brown paper. Try to buy large crumples because smaller pieces may be only fragments of whole mushrooms.

To use, soak in water at room temperature 15 minutes or more. Rinse and pick over to remove wood and dirt, especially from the thickened stump where the mushrooms were attached to the tree. Discard soaking water.

These mushrooms have little taste, but they contribute contrast in colour and texture to stir-fry mixtures and braised vegetarian dishes.

Preserved Duck Eggs (皮蛋) Pei daan. A coating of wood chips and mud encases these eggs. On the inside they are black and as solid as hard-boiled hen's eggs, with yolks that are soft, pasty and dominant. Both smell and taste have distinct, pungent, alkaline properties. Experimenters be warned: the combination of black colour, brie-like texture and aromatic taste make pei daan one of those fermented foods perhaps only enjoyed by those who have acquired the taste.

Although these eggs are sometimes called "thousand-year-old eggs," their true age is closer to 100 days. The process of preservation involves coating them with a mixture of mud and chips and curing them for a specified period, while certain bacteria transform the white to black. Thus, again, like other fermented foods, the quality of preserved eggs will vary somewhat from source to source and from batch to batch.

To use a preserved duck egg, simply crumble away the crust of mud, rinse, then shell like any hard-boiled egg. Common ways of serving preserved duck eggs are: with lean pork in congee (preparation of congee described on p. 39); fried with beaten hen's eggs in Chinese omelettes; in fish and coriander soup (p. 13); or most simply, with slices of pickled stem ginger as a snack.

Salted Duck Eggs (咸蛋) Haam daan. These eggs represent yet another way of preserving the all-too-perishable duck egg. Fresh eggs are left to soak in a special charcoal brine. The salt—but not the charcoal—permeates the egg, causing the yolk to solidify and giving the white a pleasant salty flavour. When sufficiently cured, the eggs are fished out of the black muck and dried, leaving a black powdery coat on the egg.

Judging the quality of a charcoal-encrusted salted duck egg is difficult. Once you have scraped or washed the black powder off and cracked the egg, the white should be thin, clear and watery while the yolk should be small and dark orange in colour.

The Cantonese serve these eggs hard-boiled and halved as an accompaniment to rice or congee; combine them raw with minced pork in steamed meat patties; add them to

soup for flavour; or fry them with fresh hen's eggs and a preserved duck egg in omelettes.

Sesame Oil (芝蔴油) Tsee ma yau. This is an aromatic and strong-flavoured, golden or dark-coloured oil expressed from sesame seeds. In northern parts of China it is used in large quantities with other oils as a cooking medium; the Cantonese use it only in small quantities as a seasoning. A dash or two may be added to marinades or as a final seasoning to stir-fry dishes, particularly those involving fish, bean curd or seafood or, less commonly, chicken. Used in this way, the oil will subtly enrich the dish without detectably altering its flavour.

GARLIC
Suen tau 蒜頭

APPEARANCE: Cloven or whole, garlic can be recognized at short range by its white papery husks and at long range by its inimitable smell when crushed.

QUALITY: Individual cloves should be large and full with no sign of shrivel, rot, worms or sprouting. The larger they are the easier to peel. Whole heads are usually of better quality although they sometimes harbour small worms in the central cloves.

GENERAL COMMENTS: While many Chinese are surprised Westerners use garlic, Westerners are often equally surprised to find garlic in Chinese food. In fact, garlic is a cosmopolitan condiment, more than 5,000 years old. The Chinese, as well as Europeans, Indians, Egyptians and Filipinos (but few British), employ this brash onion for its pungent, distinct and distinctive flavour, and enjoy dividends of health from the antibiotic and anti-cholesterol properties of its constituents.

Chemically, the characteristic odour and taste of garlic derive from a reaction which occurs when a certain enzyme meets a certain substrate. Any action which breaks garlic cells immediately precipitates this fragrant union. Thus, for maximum development of flavour garlic must be thoroughly minced or crushed.

Like onions, garlic may be stored in or out of the refrigerator. If the air is dry keep it in a plastic bag to prevent shrivelling; if the air is wet, keep it out of plastic to discourage sprouting.

PREPARATION: The Chinese method of crushing garlic is efficient and effective. Position unpeeled clove(s) of garlic on a chopping board, then smash it with a single, swift, firm blow of the broadside of a heavy cleaver. During crushing the husk prevents bits of garlic from scattering to all corners of the kitchen; after crushing it readily falls away from the inner clove. Further mince or crush the naked inner clove if desired.

COOKING:

Western. Wherever onions go, let a clove of garlic lead the way. Before sautéing vegetables, toss a crushed clove into the hot butter or oil. Add it to braised casseroles, marinades and salad dressings. Insert whole cloves in a leg of lamb before roasting. Make garlic bread by spreading butter in which numerous cloves of garlic have simmered on slices of French bread.

For best flavour, according to the French, never let garlic brown as it cooks.

Chinese. When stir-frying, Cantonese cooks invariably add a smashed clove of garlic to the hot oil first. When the clove is fragrant and has sufficiently "sweetened" the oil, it is removed and discarded. Garlic is also added to braised dishes, is used in sauces, and is vital to the versatile black bean sauce described earlier.

GINGER
Geung 薑

APPEARANCE: These rhizomes are golden-beige in colour with a thin, dry skin. Pieces are usually $\frac{1}{2}$–1" in diameter and vary in size from small bits to whole knobby "hands," 6" or more in length.

QUALITY: Canton ginger is reputed to be the most aromatic; Indian ginger is reputed to be the most pungent. No matter what the nationality, select rhizomes which are clear-skinned, solid and sound, with no signs of shrivelling or worms. Examine joints where rhizomes have been freshly broken: the more and larger are the hairs or fibres protruding, the older is the root. Young ginger is more tender and sweeter, but old ginger is more pungent and mellow in flavour.

GENERAL COMMENTS: In Cantonese cooking, ginger is as ancient, traditional and essential as the wok. It is used, not for its spicy pungency, but rather for its aromatic and chemical effects. When cooking fish, seafood, or organ meats ginger is added to mask or remove objectionable odours and flavours. Before cooking meat or vegetables, a crushed slice of ginger is often stirred in the hot oil first, then removed, in order to "sweeten" the oil and enhance flavours of what is cooked after. Similarly, a slice of ginger is often added to chicken and pork soups to lend a subtle piquancy to the broth.

Chemically, the two main active ingredients of ginger are a volatile oil which creates its aroma, and a water-soluble oleoresin which gives it pungency. Cooking in water or oil mutes ginger's sharpness, while mixing with acid accentuates it. Thus, for maximum hot pungency soak ginger in lemon juice or vinegar before cooking with it; for a minimum of pungency boil, braise or fry it without sour partners.

Of the rest of the rhizome, 80–90% is water, the removal of which leaves the commercial spice, ground ginger. This differs significantly from fresh Canton ginger. In the first place drying concentrates the active ingredients, particularly the pungent compounds. Secondly, most ground ginger is produced from varieties of the species much hotter than that from Canton. Thus, the commercial spice, while great for cakes and breads, is not an acceptable substitute for fresh ginger in Cantonese cooking.

PREPARATION: Peel as much of the rhizome as you will use. Cantonese cooks accomplish this by scraping the surface with the blade of a small paring knife held perpendicular to the surface being scraped. Then:
(1) For shreds, cut thinly across the grain in long diagonals and cut diagonals in fine strips.
(2) For pieces to be fried, braised or boiled, cut thickly ($\frac{1}{4}$") across the grain in diagonals and smash slices with a heavy object, such as the broadside of a cleaver.
(3) For ginger juice, grate and squeeze or press.

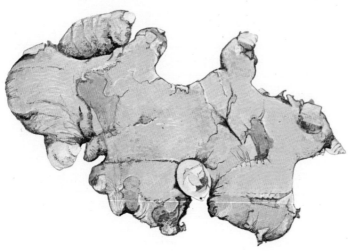

COOKING:

Shreds: Combine with vinegar to make a dip for deep-fried foods, particularly fish and seafood. You may make the dip simple or elaborate by adding minced spring onions, shallots, or chillies, soy sauce, sesame oil, sugar, wine etc., according to taste.

When steaming fish, lay the shreds generously over, under and inside the fish (as described below).

Slices: Before stir-frying vegetables or meat, toss a crushed slice of ginger in the hot oil until fragrant, then toss out and continue cooking. This procedure, while not appropriate for all foods, does enhance the flavour of many, including beansprouts, bean curd(s), lettuce and the bland summer melons.

To season soups and braised dishes, add slice(s) as desired.

Juice: Use ginger juice to marinate fish, squid, liver, shrimp or chicken 10–15 minutes before cooking. Adding a little white wine further enhances both flavour and ginger's effect.

Steamed Fish

Fish, preferably whole, necessarily mild-flavoured and very fresh
Fresh ginger, finely shredded
(Spring onions, chopped in 1–2″ lengths)
(Coriander leaves, chopped)

First, prepare apparatus for steaming, as described on p. 2.

Secondly, prepare the fish. If whole, remove scales, entrails, and head if desired (the Cantonese do not like to eat decapitated fish). Rub it lightly with salt, place on steaming dish, and liberally distribute shreds of ginger over it.

When water in the steaming pot has reached a rolling boil, place fish-&-dish on rack inside. Cover; steam 7–10 minutes or 1 minute per ounce, until done. Cooked fish have flesh which flakes easily and eyes which are opaque. Spill out any liquid which has accumulated in the dish, distribute spring onions and coriander over fish, dribble with light soy sauce, then pour hot cooked oil over all. Serve immediately.

N.B. Because it conserves delicacies of flavour and texture (not to mention energies of the cook), steaming is perhaps the best method known for cooking fresh fish. Consuming a whole steamed fish, however, can present problems—i.e., bones. The trick to eating a whole fish without killing yourself on these lurking mouthtraps is to proceed slowly and horizontally, parallel to the skeleton. A basic knowledge of fish anatomy helps; practice makes perfect.

SPRING ONIONS
Ts'ung 葱

APPEARANCE: In the West these are known as scallions or green onions. Note that the leaves are tubular, and that they are sold with the small white onion bulb still attached.

QUALITY: Select healthy plants with full-length green leaves. Often the smaller the bulbs the milder the flavour.

GENERAL COMMENTS: Spring onions are basically very young bulb onions. Any of a number of different species can be grown to produce them, with minor variations in taste. Cooks around the world use these onion greens for accent both in colour and taste. Cook them briefly—if at all—to preserve their mild, pungent flavour.

PREPARATION: Remove any dying outer leaves; wash what remains carefully, particularly at the bulb end and particularly if you plan to serve them raw. To store spring onions, wash well, trim the roots from the bulb, chop into convenient lengths, and store—preferably in a plastic box or wrapped in a paper towel in a plastic bag.

COOKING:

Western. Chop the leaves finely or snip them with scissors; toss in salads or use as a garnish for soups, casseroles, dips etc. Or, more simply, leave them whole, dip the bulb in salt, and eat as is.

Chinese. Chop or snip them into 1″ lengths; add to fried rice, fried noodles, or any dish mild in flavour and/or colour, such as fish, bean curd and egg dishes.

Fragrant Noodles

Boil noodles in water with salt and a little oil. In a serving bowl, place finely shredded fresh ginger and chopped spring onions. Pour a little hot oil over these, and season with soy sauce. When the noodles are cooked, drain them, rinse momentarily with cold water, and toss immediately in the warm flavoured oil.

SHALLOTS
Ts'ung tau 葱頭

APPEARANCE: The small, pointed shape and habit of clustering distinguish these onions. Their outer scale leaves may vary in colour from reddish-purple to brown, and the bulbs in diameter from $\frac{3}{4}''$ to $1''$. They may be sold as loose individuals or tied bunches.

QUALITY: Select these as you would any onion, avoiding those with signs of sprouts, bruises or soft rot.

GENERAL COMMENTS: This is a mild and sweet variation on the onion theme. Translation of the Chinese name accurately explains how this member fits into the family. "Ts'ung" is spring onions or scallions; "tau" means head; and, indeed, these are the bulbs which develop if salad onions are allowed to grow for two years. The French name for this sort of onion is "eschalogne," from which come both English names, "shallot" and "scallion."

PREPARATION: As with large onions, peel off dried outer skins and slice off roots. Leave whole for braising or chop as desired.

COOKING:

Western. The diminutive properties of shallots make them welcome sliced thinly in salads or braised whole in casseroles. Alternatively they may be deep-fried (or dry-fried) to make tiny onion rings for garnishing soups, casseroles, vegetables, salads etc., wherever sweet crisp onion flavour seems appropriate.

Chinese. Asian cooks commonly use these onions in the three following ways:
(1) Dry-fried until crisp to make a garnish for Indian and Indonesian curries;
(2) Braised whole with meat, poultry and/or other vegetables;
(3) Minced finely, raw, either as a substitute for spring onions in stir-fry or steamed dishes, or in marinades for meat. Cantonese cooks maintain that frozen chicken marinated with a combination of minced shallot, crushed garlic, sugar, light soy sauce, salt and cooked oil will, after steaming or frying, taste as good as fresh.

CORIANDER
Uen sai 芫茜

APPEARANCE: Fresh coriander is usually sold as plantlets, 4–6″ long, comprised of a cluster of leaves with a small taproot at the base. The leaves resemble Western parsley in colour and form, but the resemblance is not even epidermis-deep. Note that coriander leaflets are flat, thin, more or less hemispherical in shape, and distinctly scented.

QUALITY: Choose plantlets with more leaflet and less leaf stalk. Leaflets should be large, bright green and bushy.

GENERAL COMMENTS: Coriander has aided cooks since the heydays of Egypt, Rome and the Six Dynasties period in China. Its seeds, with their sweetly aromatic taste, curry Middle Eastern favour by flavouring curries, confections, breads and spirits. The leaves are more savoury and bitter, yet spicy and refreshing. The etymology of the plant's name—from the Greek "koros," meaning bug—warns of its ambivalent character. To use coriander leaves successfully, add them only where their distinctive taste will be welcome, but not overwhelming or discordant.

   Ironically enough, while the English call coriander "Chinese parsley," the Chinese name for Western parsley translates as "foreign coriander." There is an analogy here. True Western parsley and coriander are botanically distinct, albeit closely related, in a family with carrot and celery. In kitchens on their respective sides of the globe, however, both are used more for visual effect than for taste.

PREPARATION: If you intend to use fresh coriander for garnish treat it gently because it wilts irreversibly. Store in a plastic box or inflated plastic bag. When ready to use, wash quickly and shake vigorously to remove excess water. Chop as desired.

COOKING: Although Mexicans (who call it "cilantro") and Indians (who call it "hara dhania") use this green herb to season a variety of dishes and particularly to complement the heat of chillies, the Cantonese use it predominantly with fish. Coriander leaves commonly garnish steamed fish and stir-fried dishes including fish, or flavour soups as described below.

Thick Minced Beef & Coriander Soup

½ lb. beef, minced
3 egg whites, lightly beaten
2 tablespoons shredded ginger
2 tablespoons minced spring onions
2 tablespoons minced coriander
5–6 cups water or broth
2 tablespoons cornstarch

Season beef with salt, sugar, wine and soy sauce for at least 15 minutes. Bring water or broth to the boil; add beef and simmer 10 minutes. Adjust seasoning. Thicken soup with 2 tablespoons cornstarch mixed to a paste with a little water. Add egg whites to the soup while stirring vigorously with a fork into order to create fine shreds. Place ginger, onions and coriander in bottom of a tureen, or in the bottoms of bowls, and pour hot soup over; serve.

Fish & Coriander Soup

½ lb. fresh fish fillets, chopped
3 bunches of coriander, leaves chopped finely
1–2 slices fresh ginger, crushed
2 tablespoons Chinese pickled cucumber (cha gwa 茶瓜)*
(Preserved duck egg)
4–5 cups chicken stock

Shell and chop the egg as described on p. 5.

Bring the stock, with ginger, cucumber, and egg to the boil; simmer 5–10 minutes. Add fish and coriander, return to the simmer for about 5 minutes and, when fish is cooked, adjust seasoning and serve.

*For the pickled cucumber you may substitute fresh. In this case, peel the cucumber, seed, chop in small matchsticks, sprinkle lightly with salt and let rest. After 10–20 minutes, rinse, squeeze to remove excess moisture, and add to the broth with a generous pinch of sugar.

CHILLI PEPPERS
Laat jiu 辣椒

APPEARANCE: Generally, distinguish chilli peppers from sweet peppers by their small size and elongated shape, but be aware that fiery small, round, green ones do exist. Colour is not a reliable criterion because both sweet and hot peppers can be either green or red.

QUALITY: Select firm, unblemished peppers, preferably with stems. Hotness differs more with variety than with colour, although green ones tend to be hotter than red because the fruits sweeten as they ripen.

GENERAL COMMENTS: Vegetable peppers are a relatively recent addition to the cuisines of both Europe and Asia. The pepper genus, *Capsicum*, is native to South America. In 1492, Columbus introduced it to Europe (who applauded with vigour); from there it spread eastwards to India (where it usurped the culinary throne previously occupied by pepper-corns), and then to Asia and Japan.

Today, outside the Americas, two species of *Capsicum* are commonly cultivated, with myriad varieties varying in pungency from sweet Hungarian paprika to the fiery tabasco pepper. Chilli peppers and hot food are ironically appropriate for hot climates because they discourage over-eating and because they encourage blood to rush to the skin's surface (away from the chilli!), thus cooling the body from the inside out.

PREPARATION. Wash. Before continuing, determine how hot your chillis are. To ascertain the chilli's "temperature," first touch the tip of your tongue to the pepper; wait one minute. If a burning sensation develops, consider your pepper Very Hot. If you feel nothing, cut off a tiny piece and nibble; you can then label your pepper Medium or Mild, and use quantities accordingly.

For further preparation, slit the chilli(s) lengthwise; remove and discard the seeds which are reputed to be hotter than the flesh. Chop as desired—and immediately thereafter wash knife, chopping board and hands before preparing other food.

COOKING: Chillis are indispensable and integral to Mexican, Malaysian, Indian and Indonesian food, as well as Shanghai, Hunan and Szechuan foods. (Both people and food of this last province, in fact, are renowned for being spicy.) Chillis are perennial in Hong Kong markets, but seldom found in traditional Cantonese cooking and used in modern cooking primarily for colour. Restaurants use them whole as garnishes (particularly when sliced lengthwise $\frac{2}{3}$ their length, and soaked in water such that the strips of pepper curl back like flower petals), and chopped as companions for green peppers in black bean sauces. Housewives use them when preparing Indonesian and Indian curries, dishes from the fiery provinces, black bean sauces, and miscellaneous stir-fry mixtures which benefit from a touch of red colour. Commercial chilli sauces are standard condiments in both homes and restaurants for noodles, fish balls, bean curd and other similarly bland foods.

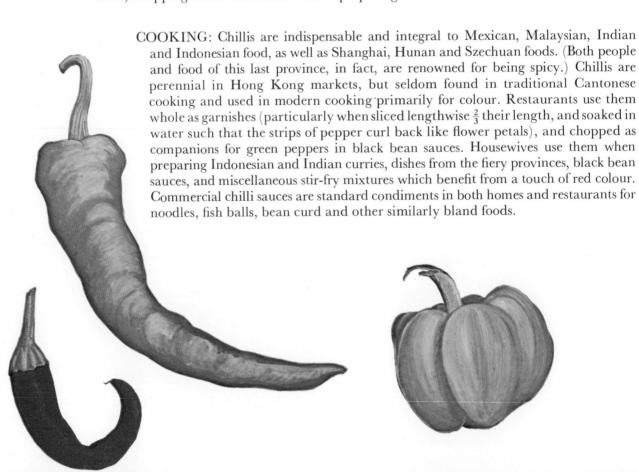

CHINESE FLOWERING CABBAGE

Choi sum 菜心

APPEARANCE: Distinguish this green vegetable by its yellow flowers and by its stems, which are uniformly $\frac{1}{4}-\frac{1}{2}''$ in diameter, 6–8″ long, and faintly grooved from tip to base.

QUALITY: The more easily your fingernail can pierce the base of the stem the more tender it is.

GENERAL COMMENTS: According to some people, this is the best of the Chinese cabbages. Stems are uniform in size and tender enough to cook without peeling. The taste is pleasant and mild for a cabbage. In Hong Kong today, this is one of the most common and popular leafy vegetables. Virtually year-round it graces bowls of noodles in simple foodstalls and garnishes platters of chicken or shark's fin at restaurant banquets.

PREPARATION: Soak in water briefly to remove dirt, particularly at the bases of leaf blades. For Cantonese cooking leave whole; otherwise chop as desired.

COOKING: No matter how you cook it, the result should be bright green to the eye and tender but crisp to the mouth.

Western. Prepare as for tender broccoli; that is, boil or steam briefly, drain, and season with salt, pepper and butter or hollandaise sauce.

Chinese. Boil in salted water with a dash of oil, drain, and serve liberally coated with oyster sauce. Stir-fry with pork, beef, chicken or squid. Or, for a fancier dish, try the following:

Winter Mushrooms and Cabbage

Winter mushrooms, preferably small whole ones, soaked
Choi sum, washed
Oyster sauce

(To further tenderize the mushrooms after soaking, you may steam them—on a dish above cooking rice or boiling soup is convenient—10–15 minutes.) Parboil the cabbage in salted water until just tender and still bright green; drain; arrange on a serving dish. When mushrooms are ready, stir-fry them in oil. Add liquid the mushrooms soaked in and water (or chicken stock) to cover the mushrooms about three-quarters. Cover and simmer 5–10 minutes. Season with oyster sauce, thicken with cornstarch, and pour mushrooms cum sauce over the cooked cabbage.

CHINESE WHITE CABBAGE
Baak choi 白菜

APPEARANCE: Of the many varieties of baak choi (also spelled "bok choy"), each differing slightly in shape, size and season, all except one can be identified by the ivory white leaf stalks. The exceptional variety, called Shanghai baak choi although it is now mainly grown in Taiwan, has light green leaf stalks, but its leaves and form are otherwise the same.

QUALITY: Select crisp-looking, unblemished plants. One variety or another is usually available all year, but the best quality and largest quantity should occur in the cooler months. Plant size is not necessarily an indicator of tenderness, but the smaller the plants within any single variety, the more tender. This is especially true during hot weather which toughens the plant quickly.

GENERAL COMMENTS: The taste, texture and versatility of this cabbage have made it popular in both Western and Eastern kitchens. The leaf stalks are succulent while the leaves are tender; both have a mild version of cabbage flavour which can stand alone or blend amicably with other savoury tastes in soup, salad or side dish.

Chinese white cabbage is known to have been grown in China since the fifth century A.D., and in Europe since the mid-eighteenth century. Since that time four major subgroups have distinguished themselves: the vegetable pictured here; the white flowering cabbage described on p. 21; the flat cabbage described on p. 20; and a cabbage known as "oil vegetable" (油菜) grown in China for its seeds which yield oil for cooking and lighting.

This particular variety of baak choi is eaten both fresh and dried. The dried form known as "choi gonn" (菜乾) is also recognized by the light colour of its leaf stalks, and seems exclusively used in soup.

PREPARATION: Separate leaves. Soak briefly in water to remove dirt trapped between stem and leaf bases. Drain; chop as desired.

COOKING: Like lettuce and spinach, this cabbage is mostly water. Thus it loses a lot of volume as it cooks, shrinking at least 50%, and it cooks quickly, within 2–3 minutes. Use strong heat otherwise it will become tough; serve it immediately to avoid it turning an unappetizing khaki-green colour.

Western. Prepare this as you would other cabbage or spinach. If tender, use it in salad. If not, boil, steam or sauté it with bacon, and season with salt, pepper and a pinch of sugar.
Chinese. The Cantonese consider this cabbage equally suitable for soup or stir-fry. When stir-frying, add a crushed clove of garlic to the oil first. Prepare it alone; with beef, chicken or pork; with Cantonese roast pork (char siu 叉燒); or with a light black bean sauce. Or simply parboil it and serve doused with oyster sauce.

When making soup, an equally wide range of supplementary ingredients can help flavour the broth. One traditional tonic soup calls for fresh and dried baak choi, a few bitter almonds, a few dried jujubes (mut jo 蜜棗) and a cleaned pig's lung. Other potential soup-mates are: pork, meat or bones, with winter melon; chicken giblets and Chinese red dates (hung jo 紅棗); ham and chicken's feet.

While all of the above soups require several hours of simmering to develop full flavour, quick versions can be made with a chicken bouillon cube, shredded pork, or minced beef as described below.

Minced Beef & Baak Choi Soup

Beef, minced and seasoned
Chinese white cabbage, washed and chopped in $\frac{1}{4}''$ cubes
Mungbean vermicelli, soaked

Use approximately equal parts by volume of beef, cabbage and dried vermicelli to 3–4 parts water in order to make a rather thick, creamy soup.

Bring water to the boil. Add vegetable. When water returns to the boil, add beef and vermicelli. Simmer until vegetable is cooked, 5–10 minutes; adjust seasoning and serve.

PEKING CABBAGE
Wong nga baak 黃芽白

APPEARANCE: Compact barrel shape, uniform yellow-white colour, and broadly ribbed leaf stalks with crinkled leaves characterize this vegetable. It comes in two sizes: long and narrow (12–18″ long, 3–4″ diameter), and short and stout (less than 12″ long, more than 5″ diameter).

QUALITY: Select heavy, compact heads with crisp, whole leaves. Long and short taste—and generally cost—the same.

GENERAL COMMENTS: Whether called Peking, Shantung, Tientsin, nappa or celery cabbage, chou de Chine, or pe-tsai, this vegetable has even more uses in cooking than it has names. Its mild cabbage taste seems to disappear as it cooks, blending with and subtly enhancing the flavours of foods it accompanies. The texture is succulent, whether stir-fried, braised or boiled.

Like common head cabbage, this cabbage keeps well. Cantonese housewives sometimes hang it for short term storage because they find it sweetens as it wilts.

PREPARATION: Wash well, particularly at the base. Chop as desired.

COOKING:

Western. Peking cabbage can be eaten raw, and has a mild, zesty pungency which lettuce lacks. The heart is particularly nice for salad. To serve it cooked, boil, steam, or braise it; blanch and roll a stuffing in individual leaves; or bake in a cream sauce au gratin.

Chinese. The Cantonese, as well as a goodly number of other Chinese, use this versatile cabbage in a wide and colourful spectrum of dishes. It is boiled in soup, braised en casserole, or stir-fried with other vegetables and meats. Its sponge-like ability to absorb flavours and its pleasant texture make it equally compatible with rich flavours—as, for instance, beneath a highly flavoured sauce such as the oyster beef described on p. 95—or with delicate ones, such as fish and bean curd. Blanched leaves may be rolled with a fresh shrimp or minced pork filling, and steamed or braised. When stir-frying, Peking cabbage can be included to flavourful advantage in virtually any mixture, or simply served on its own.

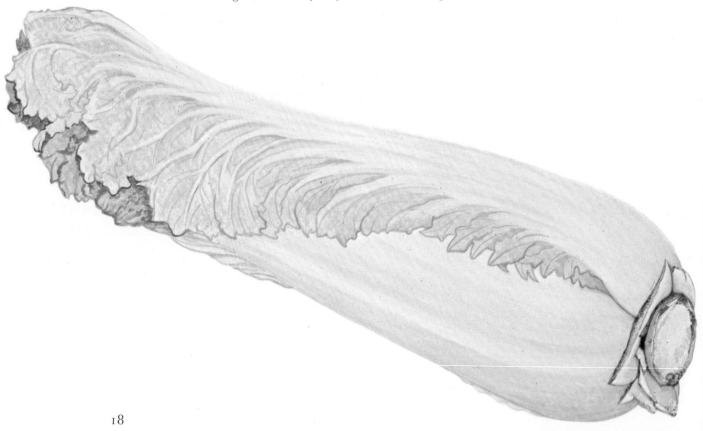

Peking Cabbage Casserole

Peking cabbage, washed, sliced diagonally, $\frac{1}{2}''$ wide
Dried shrimps, soaked
Mungbean vermicelli, soaked
Spring onions, chopped in $1''$ lengths
Bean curd, cubed
Fish balls
Winter mushrooms, soaked
Chicken stock

In large braising pot, fry shrimps in oil over medium heat, 3–4 minutes. Add cabbage and remaining ingredients with water or light stock just to cover. Cover the pot and braise 15–30 minutes to blend flavours. Adjust seasoning and serve.

As for quantities, use about 1 tablespoon dried shrimp with about 2 cups cabbage; add any of the other ingredients according to taste and availability.

To make a meal, serve this with a selection of richly tasty Chinese meats, such as Cantonese barbecued pork (char siu), spiced duck or Chinese sausage (lap cheung), plus plain steamed rice and dipping dishes of soy sauce and chilli sauce for the bean curd and fish balls.

Cabbage and Ham

Peking cabbage, cut in diagonal slices $\frac{1}{2}''$ wide
Garlic
Ham, shredded
Chicken stock (or bouillon cube)

Stir-fry cabbage until cooked; remove to serving dish. Heat a little more oil, fry a crushed clove of garlic until fragrant; remove. Add ham, then stock; simmer briefly. Adjust seasoning with salt and white pepper, thicken with cornstarch and pour sauce over cabbage.

CHINESE FLAT CABBAGE
Taai goo choi 太古菜

APPEARANCE: This cabbage grows like a flat, round plate or saucer, only a few inches tall but 5–14″ in diameter. The leaf stalks have the familiar ivory colour of Chinese white cabbage, baak choi.

QUALITY: Smaller plants with many young leaves clustered at the centre are the best.

GENERAL COMMENTS: This stout cabbage is popular among farmers, particularly in the vicinity of Shanghai, because it withstands heavy snow and frost. When cooked, its texture is slightly tougher than upright baak choi and its taste is also somewhat stronger.

PREPARATION: Wash, giving special attention to the leaf bases.

COOKING: The differences between this cabbage and baak choi are purely superficial. Prepare this in any and all ways described for its more common cousin.

CHINESE KALE
Gaai laan 芥蘭

APPEARANCE: Distinguish this from other cabbages by its white flowers, the white haze on its leaves, and its overall stoutness. Unlike Chinese flowering cabbage, this vegetable has stems which are smooth, not grooved, and which measure $\frac{1}{2}-\frac{3}{4}''$ or more in diameter.

QUALITY: Select plants with unblemished leaves, more flowers in bud than in bloom, and with thick stalks. In preparing this vegetable for cooking, the stems must often be peeled so stems of large diameter require less peeling per serving.

GENERAL COMMENTS: The leaves of this vegetable are rather tougher in texture and stronger in taste than Chinese flowering cabbage; however, the stem offers compensation for these shortcomings because its pith is a tender, succulent and flavourful delicacy.

PREPARATION: Soak briefly in water to remove dirt. Remove leaves and chop them coarsely. Peel the fibrous outer layer from the stems and chop what remains into pieces of uniform size for even cooking.

COOKING:
Western. Prepare as you would broccoli. Steam or boil it, chopped or as whole stalks, in a minimum of water; drain, season with salt, pepper and butter, or with a cheese or hollandaise sauce.
Chinese. Stir-frying seems to tenderize and enhance the good points of this vegetable better than boiling. Stir-fry it alone, with shredded pork, or with chicken meat or giblets, adding a dash of cooking wine and a pinch of sugar when the vegetable is half-cooked.

SWATOW MUSTARD CABBAGE
Daai gaai choi 大芥菜

APPEARANCE: This vegetable resembles head lettuce in size and shape but differs in that the leaves wrapping the heart are all stalk. Typically the leaf blades have been removed, presumably because they are not fit for human consumption, leaving only broad midrib.

QUALITY: Choose heavy heads with no sign of rot, particularly on the cut surfaces.

GENERAL COMMENTS: This type of mustard cabbage has a particularly strong and pungent flavour. Some is cooked fresh, but most of the crop is salted—just as the Germans salt head cabbage to make sauerkraut—to make the preserved vegetable known as "haam suen choi" 咸酸菜 (literal translation: salted-sour vegetable).

PREPARATION: Wash heads well, particularly at the leaf bases. Chop whole head crosswise in slices or chunks.

COOKING: For Cantonese, fresh daai gaai choi is strictly soup material, and wise Western cooks follow their example. As with other cabbages, bring water to a rolling boil before adding the vegetable and simmer at least one hour. To flavour the broth, the Cantonese use pork bones, pork shin, barbecued roast duck or a salted egg. Beef, carrot and a bay leaf work equally well.

Duck Soup

$\frac{1}{4}-\frac{1}{2}$ of a whole barbecued roast duck (siu ngop 燒鴨)
2–3 heads Swatow mustard cabbage, chopped in chunks
1–2 slices fresh ginger, crushed.

Separate meat from bones of the duck. In large pot put the bones and ginger with approximately three times as much water by volume as you have ingredients. Bring to a boil; add cabbage; simmer 2–3 hours. At least 15 minutes before serving, add duck meat. Just before serving adjust seasoning with salt or light soy sauce.

Haam suen choi (咸酸菜), as illustrated, has the form of a fresh cabbage head and the colour of a pickled green olive. Furthermore, it has the smooth but crunchy texture and sour tang of good sauerkraut or good dill pickles. Stir-fry it with beef, pork, eel or squid. Before cooking rinse the vegetable well in water; during cooking season it with a pinch of sugar and a dash of vinegar; finally bind it all together with a light cornstarch sauce.

Haam Suen Choi Chau Yau Yue

Haam suen choi	Vinegar
Fresh squid	Sugar
Fermented black beans	Cornstarch
Garlic	

Use approximately equal parts by volume of vegetable and squid; use about 1 tablespoon of black beans for 2–3 cups of ingredients.

Lightly mash black beans with a crushed clove or two of garlic.

Prepare vegetable by rinsing it in water to remove excess salt. Squeeze fairly dry; chop in bite-size pieces,

Prepare squid as follows: Remove ink sack. Decapitate; discard head but save tendrils. From the body remaining, remove the single central bone and peel away the purple-spotted skin. Rinse. Lay skin-side down on chopping board and score it with a knife in a grid pattern (for decorative effect when cooked, otherwise unnecessary). Chop body into bite-sized rectangles.

To cook, first lightly toss and cook haam suen choi in a hot, dry wok. Remove. Add oil, when hot, add black beans and garlic. When fragrant and very hot, add squid. Stir and cook until the pieces curl and turn white. Add haam suen choi with a dash of water and a hefty pinch of sugar. Braise briefly while you mix cornstarch with vinegar-and-water to a paste. Add this to thicken the sauce, and serve.

This dish may be served alone, or as a sauce over any bland vegetable, such as jicama, kohlrabi, any of the melons, etc.

BAMBOO MUSTARD CABBAGE
Chuk gaai choi 竹芥菜

APPEARANCE: The single most reliable characteristic for identifying mustard cabbages is the ribbed, green leaf stalk with leaf blade extending almost to the base. Like lettuce, some varieties form heads while others grow in stalks. The variety illustrated here is distinguished by notched edges on its leaf blades and medium 8–12″ size.

QUALITY: Select healthy, unblemished, bushy plants.

GENERAL COMMENTS: Mustard cabbage has been nourishing Chinese people (and their livestock) since before the beginning of recorded agricultural history. It grows best in the humid but temperate region near the Yangtse River, and hence is eaten most by people of Szechuan and Swatow.

Generally speaking, mustard cabbage is robust peasant fare rather than esteemed delicacy. One of the most pungent cabbages known, it is unpleasantly strong in a fresh, raw state. After parboiling, however, the leafstalks are tender and succulent, with only a vestige of their former pungency and a pleasant predisposition for absorbing other flavours.

PREPARATION: Wash, drain, chop. Use as is for soup. Before stir-frying, parboil or blanch it in rapidly boiling water 2–3 minutes.

COOKING:

Western. Cook this vegetable as you would the leaves of head cabbage. Add it in small quantities with other vegetables to beef or pork bone soups. Or boil, drain, season and serve as a side dish.

Chinese. For soup, boil the cabbage with chicken, pork or beef bones (using 1 part vegetable to 3–4 parts water) for several hours or until the broth is well flavoured. Cantonese cooks insist that the water must be boiling briskly as the vegetable goes in, and that a slice of fresh ginger must go in as well.

As a side dish, the easiest way to prepare gaai choi is to serve it immediately after blanching, drained, dribbled with a little cooked oil and a lot of oyster sauce. When stir-frying, add a smashed slice of fresh ginger to the oil before adding the (parboiled) vegetable. Stir-fry it with pork, beef, chicken or shrimp, or with a garlic-black bean sauce.

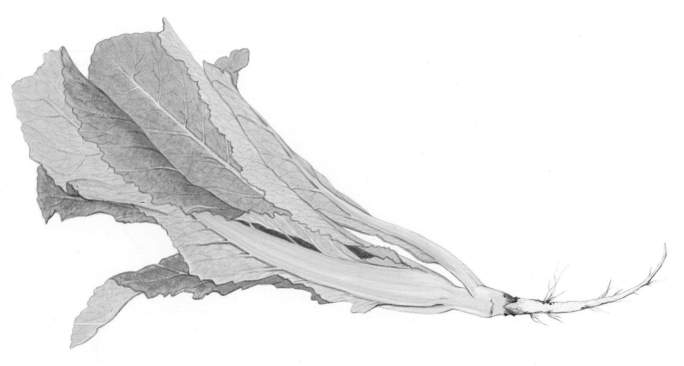

SOW CABBAGE
Jiu la choi 豬乸菜

APPEARANCE: Measuring some 12–18″ in length, this is probably the longest leafy vegetable in the market. To distinguish it from the other mustard greens which also have wide,
ribbed leafstalks, note that the leaves of this one have smooth edges and that the leaf bases
broadly wrap more than half way around the stem. Other subtle characteristics separate
the two but defy description.
(N.B. Differentiation is not critical because all mustard cabbages may be cooked in the
same ways.)

QUALITY: Choose stalks with large, well-formed leaf midribs because this is the best part
of the vegetable for eating.

GENERAL COMMENTS: Of the three mustard cabbages described here—chuk gaai
choi, daai gaai choi, and jiu la choi—this has the best flavour and is the first choice for serving
as a vegetable side dish rather than for boiling in soup. The midrib is succulent without
being stringy and the taste blends amenably with other robust flavours.

PREPARATION: Separate leaves and wash well; chop leaves crosswise in $\frac{1}{2}$″ lengths. Bring
water to a rolling boil; add leaves; boil 1–2 minutes, drain and rinse with cool water.

COOKING:
Western. Sauté with garlic in bacon drippings; or in butter with dill or caraway seeds;
or sauté, season with salt, pepper and a pinch of sugar, and toss with a dollop of sour cream.
Chinese. Most Cantonese agree that the best way to prepare this cabbage is to stir-fry it
parboiled, with garlic and black beans, with or without pork.

HEAD CABBAGE
Yeh choi 椰菜

APPEARANCE: This vegetable is a solid, yellow-white ball of overlapping, tightly clasping leaves; diameters vary from 6″ to 12″.

QUALITY: Heads should be heavy, compact and without signs of rot at the stem, or worm holes, or of flowering. Green leaves are more nutritious, but white ones are more tender.

GENERAL COMMENTS: This cabbage originated in Europe and has only relatively recently closed ranks with its Asian relatives. While traditional Chinese cooks still consider it foreigners' food, younger chefs have found it a place in modern Chinese cuisine. East or west, head cabbage is easy to grow, easy to transport from field to market, and easy to store (i.e. economical), as well as nutritious and potentially delicious. The Cantonese name "yeh choi" literally means "coconut vegetable," and presumably refers both to its appearance and to the mild, nutty crunch of the leaves eaten raw or lightly cooked.

    Solid, cleanly-cut heads of cabbage, stored in a dry plastic bag in the refrigerator, should keep at least a month without deterioration.

COOKING:

Western. The extensive repertoire of Western recipes for cabbage reflects its easy and historically lengthy culture. In England, cabbage boiled with corned beef is a venerated tradition; shredded raw cabbage and carrot comprise the American classic, coleslaw. French cooks wrap seasoned meat stuffing in cabbage leaves for braising, while Germans salt it to make sauerkraut.

    To summarize, cabbage may be boiled, braised, stuffed, pickled, sautéd, or served raw as salad.

Chinese. Stir-frying is an excellent method of cooking cabbage because it brings out maximum sweetness with a minimum of the unpleasant pungency in smell and taste of overcooked cabbage. Stir-fry it on its own, seasoned only with salt; or with shredded beef, pork or chicken; or with shrimp (fresh or dried) and mungbean vermicelli; or serve it under a braised meat sauce or oyster sauce.

Cabbage, Shrimp and Vermicelli

1 tablespoon dried shrimp, soaked
1 handful mungbean vermicelli, soaked
3–4 cups coarsely shredded cabbage
1 slice fresh ginger, crushed

With kitchen scissors or a knife, cut wet vermicelli into 4–5″ lengths for easier eating later; drain it. Heat oil in wok, add the ginger, remove and add shrimp. Fry them 3–4 minutes until fragrant; remove. Add more oil if necessary, and when quite hot, stir-fry cabbage. Season with salt, a pinch of sugar, a dash of wine; add a little water to create steam; cover and cook. When cabbage is almost done, return shrimps with vermicelli; toss and cook to blend flavours and to reduce any liquid remaining. Adjust seasoning and serve.

WATERCRESS
Sai yeung choi 西洋菜

APPEARANCE: In the market this vegetable appears in disorderly heaps. Distinguish it by the red-purple tint and irregular shape of its small leaves, and by its curved hollow stems.

QUALITY: Tender green tips are best; buy as little of the thicker, tougher, lower stems as possible.

GENERAL COMMENTS: Apparently, Hong Kong was responsible for introducing this plant to China, around the turn of the twentieth century. Being rather easy to grow and of a familiar cabbage flavour, it has since become quite common and popular among Cantonese (who, despite the best British advice to serve it raw, consistently boil the living daylights out of it in soup).

Watercress has a pungent taste, reminiscent of its cabbage relations yet decidedly different, whether raw or cooked. Raw young shoots are tender, crisp and sharp in flavour; boiled shoots are limp and stringy, but yield a mellowed, flavourful broth.

PREPARATION: Soak in water briefly and wash carefully. Chop coarsely, discarding tough lower stems.

COOKING:

Western. Western cooks add this green to salads, include it in sandwiches (especially with cream cheese to dampen its zing), and purée it to make a refreshing soup.

Chinese. The Cantonese concede that stir-frying this green is possible, but most commonly they boil it in a variation of the following soup:

Pork & Watercress Soup

Pork: meat and/or bones and/or intestines
Watercress, washed, chopped coarsely if at all
(Dried duck's kidney 乾鴨腎)
(Dried tangerine peel 乾柑皮)
(Chinese almonds 南北杏)

Bring water and pork to a rolling boil; add watercress and other ingredients as desired. Simmer several hours until broth is well-flavoured. Season with salt and serve.

N.B.   For a quicker soup, bring chicken broth to the boil, add watercress, and simmer until the cress has turned olive green, about 30 minutes.

FLOWERING CHINESE CHIVES
Gau choi fa 韮菜花; **Gau choi sum** 韮菜心

APPEARANCE: As the name explains, this vegetable is the flower ("fa") of Chinese chives ("gau choi"). Identify them in the market as tubular green stems 8–10″ long with a single, conical bud at the tip of each.

QUALITY: The smaller, harder and tighter the flower head, the younger the stalk and the more tender it is likely to be. Those with open flowers are considered too old to eat.

GENERAL COMMENTS: Like spring onions and Chinese chives, gau choi fa have a basic onion taste. The stalks are thin and stiff as needles to behold (also hold), yet are tender and mild to eat. Cooked, they seem to retain their bright green colour better than spring onions.

PREPARATION: Wash; chop in 2″ lengths or as desired, discarding lowest, toughest portions of stems. Some cooks advocate removing the flower buds; others leave them on, with no unsavoury consequences.

COOKING:

Western. Mince; then toss in salads, beat into omelettes, sprinkle on soup, mix in dips—in other words, use wherever a dash of colour and onion flavour are desired.

Chinese. The Cantonese usually chop this green in $1\frac{1}{2}$–2″ lengths and stir-fry it, particularly with beef. It is also stir-fried on its own and served as a side dish with seafood, or braised with bean curd. Use gau choi fa as a general substitute for spring onions.

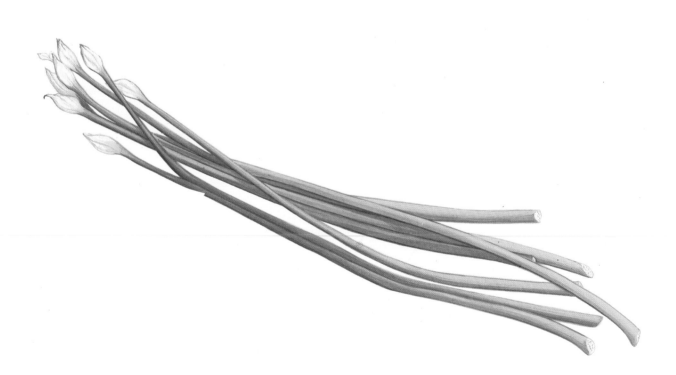

BLANCHED CHINESE CHIVES
Gau wong 韮黃

APPEARANCE: These are Chinese chives (gau choi p. 31) which have been grown in the dark. They appear in the market as limp mounds of flat leaves 10–12″ long, identical to gau choi in every respect except colour.

QUALITY: Select only fresh leaves with no signs of decay.

GENERAL COMMENTS: The blanching process (i.e., growing the plants in the dark) discourages the formation of chlorophyll and results in languishing weak plants. In the context of the dinner table this means tender; in the context of the refrigerator this means a short, 1–2 day shelf life.

PREPARATION: Rinse in water, drain and use immediately or pat dry with a towel and store in a plastic box.

COOKING:
Western. Use as you would chives, but with more discretion in deference to their stronger taste. Toss in salads, beat into omelettes, sprinkle on soups, etc.
Chinese. The customary way of serving gau wong is to chop them in 2″ lengths and combine them with noodles, either in soup or fried. They may also be included in fillings for spring rolls or wonton as well as in virtually any stir-fry mixture.

CHINESE CHIVES
Gau choi 韮菜

APPEARANCE: These are long, flat green leaves, about $\frac{1}{4}''$ wide and always sold as leaves only, never with a bulb.

QUALITY: Uniformly dark green leaves are good; often the shorter they are the younger and thus the more tender and mild in taste.

GENERAL COMMENTS: Gau choi has a stronger taste and a tougher, more fibrous texture than either spring onions or true chives. Its flat, rather than tubular, leaves indicate that it belongs to the garlic clan of the onion family; nevertheless, the name "Chinese chives" is appropriate because East Asian peoples use—and for centuries have used— these greens in much the same way Westerners use true chives.

PREPARATION: Wash and air- or blot dry with a paper towel. Chop, discarding the tough tips, and store them like spring onions: preferably in a plastic box or wrapped in a paper towel in a plastic bag. Plan to use them within 2–3 days because, without bulbs, they will not keep as well as spring onions.

COOKING:

Western. Chop finely in view of their tough texture, and use sparingly in deference to their stronger taste but in the same way as spring onions, i.e., in salads, soups, omelettes, dips, herb butters, etc.

Chinese. Traditional Cantonese cooks serve gau choi simmered in a little broth with squares of coagulated pig's or chicken's blood. (These squares, sold from tubs of water in market or meat stalls, have the colour of cooked liver, the texture of bean curd, and little taste.) Alternatively, other Cantonese cooks parboil gau choi and serve it alone as a vegetable, or braised, as described below:

Bo Jai Choi

Bean curd
Lean pork, shredded
Winter mushrooms, soaked
Gau choi, cut in 2″ lengths

In braising pot, lightly fry bean curd. Add remaining ingredients, with water or light stock to half cover. Simmer gently 15–30 minutes; season with soy sauce and a dash of oyster sauce and serve.

31

WATER SPINACH
Ong choi 甕菜

APPEARANCE: Identify ong choi by its jointed hollow stems and arrowhead-shaped leaves. The species comprises two varieties which differ slightly in colour, leaf shape and form. The variety illustrated here is "seui ong choi," and has relatively thick stems, a light green colour, and larger leaves. The other variety, "gonn ong choi," has smaller, $\frac{1}{2}''$ diameter stems, medium-green colour, and abundant, narrower leaves.

QUALITY: Within either variety the shorter the stalks and the larger the leaves at the tip, the more tender the mouthfuls.

GENERAL COMMENTS: This vegetable tastes mildly like spinach. Its most outstanding attribute is the contrast in texture between crunchy stem and limp leaves when cooked. In other parts of the tropics, ong choi is eaten raw; however, this can only be recommended if it has been grown in clean water and has been washed well.

In serving ong choi two consequences of its high water content should be considered. First, use what you buy within 2–3 days because the leaves quickly yellow and succumb to soggy rot. Secondly, expect it to shrink to about one-third of its original volume by the time it is cooked.

PREPARATION: Wash by soaking briefly in water; discard lowest 1–2″ of stems which are too tough to eat. Chop as desired, keeping stems and leaves roughly separate so that tougher stems may be cooked first, longer.

COOKING:

Western. Treat as you would ordinary spinach: sauté with butter and garlic, or with bacon and toss with a little vinegar and sugar; or serve creamed. A piquant mustard complements this vegetable nicely.

Chinese. Although other Asians serve water spinach in a variety of ways—in soup, batter-fried, raw, etc.—the Cantonese exclusively stir-fry it, using garlic and either white fermented bean curd or shrimp sauce for flavour. The slight tang of fermentation seems to complement the taste of the vegetable remarkably well, while stir-frying imparts a welcome richness to the final dish.

Stir-fried Water Spinach

1 clove garlic, crushed
Seasoning (in suggested quantities only: alter according to taste after experiment):
1 cube white fermented bean curd (foo yue 腐乳)
OR 1 teaspoon dried shrimp cake (ha goe 蝦糕)
OR 1 tablespoon shrimp sauce (ha jeung 蝦醬)
½ catty water spinach

In hot oil in wok fry garlic until fragrant; remove and discard. Add vegetable: stems first; stir and toss one minute, then add leaves. Continue to toss until wilted. Add desired seasoning plus a pinch of sugar and a splash of water if it seems appropriate; cover and cook until done. This spinach cooks quickly so the entire operation should take no more than 3–4 minutes over good, strong heat. There should be no need to add salt because all of the suggested seasonings are naturally salty.

CHINESE SPINACH

Een choi 莧菜

APPEARANCE: As illustrated, this vegetable is usually sold as shoot with root. Its broad oval leaves cluster limply at the tips of the stems, while flower stalks, if present, are bumpy green spikes several inches long. One variety has leaves with red centres.

QUALITY: Select plants with many and large leaves. The red-leaved type is sometimes considered more choice, but seems to taste and cost the same.

GENERAL COMMENTS: Peoples of Southeast Asia have cultivated this plant and its near botanical relatives for centuries, while temperate zone folks, believing them to be weeds, have campaigned to eradicate them. As the name suggests, the Chinese use this vegetable as Westerners use spinach, either in soup or as a side dish. Both leaves and stems become limp when cooked; the taste is mild but distinct and different.

PREPARATION: Soak the leaves in water briefly to remove grit. Discard the roots and lowest inch or so of tough stem. Chop in 2″ lengths for Chinese cooking, or as desired.

COOKING:
Western. Cook this vegetable as you would spinach. Either boil it or steam it briefly, drain, and season; sauté it with bacon; bake it au gratin with cheese or seafood; or serve it in a cream sauce.
Chinese. Cantonese cooks stir-fry this green with garlic; or use it to prepare a quick soup, as described below.

Chinese Spinach Soup

Sauté crushed garlic in a little oil. Add water or light stock, and bring to the boil. Add the prepared spinach, using approximately equal volumes of water and fresh vegetable. Simmer several minutes; season with salt and a dash of cooked oil; serve.

CHINESE BOX THORN
Gau gei choi 枸杞菜

APPEARANCE: Identify this vegetable by its straight, stout, unbranched stems, closely covered with small oval leaves and, in one species, thorns. The branches usually measure 10–14″ long, have stems like rods, and more or less resemble slim feather dusters.

QUALITY: The main criterion is a bushy green look of healthy vigour.

GENERAL COMMENTS: This vegetable belongs to a family (the *Solanaceae*) of considerable diversity and economic importance. Different members, at different times and in different countries, have been used for their ornamental flowers (petunia), edible fruits (tomato), or drug-laden leaves (tobacco). Thus, both the tomato and eggplant were first grown in Europe as ornamentals. Similarly, this plant, while being cultivated for food in Asia and Africa, was first grown in England as an ornamental. A related species known as matrimony vine is still grown for food in southern Europe. (In England the Chinese box thorn has now escaped the confines of gardens and become a naturalized weed.)

As the dark green colour of gau gei leaves suggests, they are rich in protein, calcium and iron. As their thin texture suggests, they go quite limp when cooked.

PREPARATION: First check for thorns; then defoliate the stems by grasping the tip with one hand and running your hand down its length, avoiding thorns. Save the leaves, discard the stems.

COOKING:

Western. In the Chinese tradition, make soup. Either simply boil the leaves briefly in chicken broth, or purée them to create a cream soup.

Chinese. For the Cantonese, this is strictly soup material, usually used with pork liver. The thin leaves cook almost as quickly as the liver, and both impart different but distinct flavours to the broth.

Box Thorn Soup

$\frac{1}{2}$ cup pork liver, fresh, thinly sliced seasoned with
  sugar, salt, cornstarch and fresh ginger juice
4 cups box thorn leaves
5–6 cups water or light stock

Heat a small amount of oil in a saucepan. Add the box thorn leaves and stir until wilted. Add water or stock; bring to the boil and simmer about 5 minutes. Add liver, and continue to simmer 2–3 minutes until liver is just cooked. Season with salt and a liberal dash of pepper and serve.

SLIPPERY VEGETABLE
Saan choi 潺菜

APPEARANCE: Only sharp eyes will distinguish this vegetable from the cabbages. Note that both stems and leaves have the same bright green colour; that the leaves themselves are broad in shape, rather rubbery to the touch; and that no flowers are present. Finally and particularly, note the characteristically wide U-shape with which the leaf stalks join the stem.

QUALITY: Select young tender plants, characterized by bright colour, lack of blemishes and large leaves.

GENERAL COMMENTS: A better translation of the Chinese word "saan" 潺 is not slippery, but mucilaginous, and this second adjective quite accurately describes the eating texture of this vegetable. The taste is mild and inoffensive, but the feeling of it in one's mouth is not universally popular.

 Elsewhere in Southeast Asia saan choi is known as Ceylon or Indian spinach. The above name, a translation of the Cantonese, seems more descriptively appropriate because the vegetable is also reputed to be a mild laxative.

PREPARATION: Wash the leaves well; chop stem and leaves coarsely.

COOKING: Most Asians, including the Cantonese, seem to use saan choi almost exclusively in soup. Americans might use it as a substitute for okra, another mucilaginous vegetable, in Louisiana gumbo dishes.

Slippery Soup

Heat a small amount of oil in a saucepan. Add a slice of fresh ginger; when fragrant, add water or chicken stock and bring to the boil. Add saan choi, using about 1 cup of vegetable per 1–2 cups of liquid; fresh bean curd may go in as well. Simmer 5–10 minutes, season with salt and white pepper, and serve.

 Instead of salt, you may add a fresh salted duck egg (haam daan 咸蛋), one egg per 3–4 cups of soup, to impart flavour, variety and protein to the final brew.

36

PEA SHOOTS
Dau miu 豆苗

APPEARANCE: In the market this vegetable appears in small, rather sorry-looking heaps. Each shoot is a short limp stem bearing small, oval leaflets, often with a waxy-white bloom and curling tendrils.

QUALITY: Buy only if they seem freshly picked and have the white-blushing, many-tendrilled look of youth.

GENERAL COMMENTS: Pleasant taste, tender texture, bright colour and scarcity are the qualities which give pea shoots their gastronomic status. Botanically, these shoots are the growing tips of ordinary green pea plants. Horticulturally, the plants are grown as creepers rather than upright vines, and are prevented from flowering or fruiting. Thus, lacking adult fibre, the shoots wilt as soon as they are picked and begin to deteriorate almost as quickly. Use dau miu within 2–3 days of purchase (or plucking).

PREPARATION: Wash and drain.

COOKING:

Western. Steam or sauté in butter, and season with salt and pepper. Substitute for spinach in florentine dishes, particularly those with seafood. Bake in white sauce au gratin, or serve with a cream, cheese, or mustard sauce.

Chinese. Because of their expense and scarcity, pea shoots are a vegetable for special occasions. In homes they may be boiled quickly in broth flavoured with lean pork and liver, or simply stir-fried with fresh ginger. Restaurants are more apt to serve them with another delicacy such as snake or crab meat, as described below.

Haai Pa-Dau Miu

3–4 cups pea shoots
1 cup crab meat, flaked or shredded
1 egg white, lightly beaten
1 cup light stock (or water plus chicken bouillon cube)
(White wine or cooking sherry)
(Sesame oil)

With a minimum of oil, stir-fry pea shoots and mound on serving dish. In wok or saucepan combine stock with 1 tablespoon cornstarch; heat, stirring constantly. As sauce thickens, add crabmeat and season with (a dash of sesame oil, a dash of wine) salt and white pepper. Simmer gently a moment or two. When mixture seems thoroughly cooked, add egg white as you stir vigorously to break the white into shreds as it coagulates. Adjust seasoning, pour sauce over shoots, and serve.

N.B. For the crabmeat you may substitute shrimp, shrimpballs, fishballs or shreds of cooked chicken (but then you mustn't call it "Haai Pa"-Dau Miu).

LETTUCE
Saang choi 生菜

APPEARANCE: Leaf lettuce, as illustrated, comes in many varieties. Leaves may vary in shape from broad to narrow, with edges jagged or smooth. Note, however, that all lack distinct leaf stalks and have a rather thin texture. These characteristics, plus its overall lighter colour and smaller size, distinguish lettuce from the mustard cabbages.

QUALITY: Hot weather and/or old age cause lettuce plants to produce flower stalks, bitter chemicals and tough leaves. Thus, bunches with short stems, large leaves and no evidence of flower stalks will be the sweetest and most tender.

GENERAL COMMENTS: The botanical genus of lettuce is *Lactuca*, a name which derives from the Latin name for milk, *lac*, and which refers to the white sap characteristic of all its species. *L. sativa*, the widely cultivated salad crop of today, probably originated in the Middle East. It may have been grown for its seeds, was definitely used for its narcotic sap, and first appeared on the dinner table in Persia around 550 B.C. Some thousand years later it reached China.

If species diversity is any measure of national taste preferences, Europeans have consistently enjoyed eating lettuce more than Asians. (Asian varieties are perhaps less crisp or harder to grow.) In A.D. 79 Pliny described nine varieties of leaf lettuce; by 1543 the species had come to a head; by 1765 English gardens boasted 18 varieties; and today more than five times that number exist.

The myriad of lactucal varieties can be reduced to four main groups: head lettuces; cos or romaine lettuces; leaf lettuces; and stem lettuce (see p. 73). Cos lettuce is much like Peking cabbage in form, size and texture. Head and leaf lettuces differ slightly in taste and greatly in texture. The former is tender, crisp, but virtually tasteless, while the latter tends to be tougher but more flavourful.

As mentioned above, the Chinese have been growing lettuce—both *L. sativa* and their own species, *L. indica*—for centuries. Superstition, even more than nutrition, may explain why. The Chinese name for lettuce, 生菜, pronounced "saang choi" in Cantonese, is a homonym: the word "choi" can mean either vegetable or money depending on the tone with which you say it, while "saang" can mean fresh or first. Thus, lettuce is an auspicious vegetable. It is associated with riches and served on birthdays, New Year's Day—as well as many other days!—to ensure future prosperity.

PREPARATION: Separate leaves; wash thoroughly.

COOKING: Head and leaf lettuce are interchangeable, raw or cooked, although results differ according to their differences of taste and texture. Whenever cooking lettuce of any sort, (1) do it quickly, over high heat, in order to serve it green, sweet and crunchy; and (2) expect great shrinkage.

Western. Raw lettuce is the foundation of tossed salad, and a mixed salad of leaf and head lettuces combines the best of taste and texture in both worlds. Cooked lettuce is unheard of in contemporary Western cuisine, although exposure to Chinese cooking may help clear the West's ears. In particular, lettuce may substitute for grape leaves in making Greek dolma or for cabbage leaves in making stuffed ground meat rolls.

Chinese. The seemingly unlimited variety of ways in which the Cantonese serve lettuce can be reduced to three categories: as envelopes for "saang choi bau" described below; as a vegetable; in soup.

As a vegetable, lettuce may be parboiled or stir-fried: with only ginger and garlic; with fresh mushrooms; with dried winter mushrooms; with chicken, beef, pork, liver or other viscera. It may garnish a platter or support a richly flavoured sauce of braised scallops, of deep-fried pigeon eggs, of oysters (i.e. oyster sauce) or of fresh shrimp and spring onions or chives. Lettuce, fish and bean curd are a common combination of complementary tastes and textures which comes to mouth as soup, congee (see below), stew and stir-fry dishes.

For soup, use virtually any combination of the ingredients mentioned above to flavour the broth, then add the lettuce last in order to cook it only briefly before serving. (See recipe for bean curd, p. 52.)

Fresh Fish Congee

Rice: preferably short grain, white rice (long-grain and brown do not disintegrate properly). Use approximately $\frac{1}{4}$ cup per serving.
(1–2 dried scallops (gong yue 江瑤柱), soaked)
(Chicken bones or meat)
In quantities to taste:
    Fish fillet of mild flavour and best quality, cut in small pieces
    Lettuce, thinly shredded
    Ginger, very finely shredded
    Spring onions, minced

To make congee, put rice in large pot with approximately 8–10 times as much water as rice; add scallops and chicken if desired. Bring to a boil and simmer 2–3 hours until porridge is thick and individual rice grains have disintegrated. During cooking, rice foam will spew out the top unless steam can escape naturally. Chinese pots have a hole in the lid to provide this necessary ventilation. With a rice cooker or saucepan, prop the lid open by sandwiching a wooden chopstick between rim and lid to one side of pot. Alternatively, modern Cantonese cooks recommend using a crockpot, on lowest setting, overnight.

When congee has reached the creamy consistency of oat porridge or pea soup, it is ready. Add fish; when congee returns to the boil, add lettuce. Season with salt, white pepper and a little cooked oil. As soon as fish and lettuce are cooked, serve. At the table provide ginger, spring onions and light soy sauce for each diner to sprinkle on or dribble into his bowl as desired.

N.B. Although the Cantonese usually combine lettuce only with fish in congee, you can, of course, combine it with anything. Congee is simply a thick soup base which can be—and is—flavoured with an endless variety and combination of ingredients: shreds of beef, pork or chicken; giblets; preserved duck eggs; beef, shrimp, or fish-balls; salted eggs etc. (Turkey Congee is said to be a traditional delicacy found only in certain American homes towards the end of November.)

Birthday Lettuce

Lettuce, chopped or torn into pieces
Winter mushrooms, soaked
Bean curd, each large square quartered
Oyster sauce

In a minimum of very hot oil, stir-fry lettuce and remove. Heat more oil, season it with crushed pieces of garlic and ginger, then brown bean curd on all sides. Finally add mushrooms, any liquid which has accumulated under the lettuce, mushroom-soaking liquid, and a generous splash of oyster sauce. Cover; braise 3–4 minutes. Uncover; thicken sauce with a cornstarch paste, season with soy sauce and, after a total of approximately 6 minutes, scoop onto lettuce and serve.

Meal in a Leaf

The history of this dish is obscure. Botanical experts at the University of Hong Kong believe that it is of recent origin, inspired by the arrival in Hong Kong of American "Bud" lettuce and by acceptance of the custom of eating it raw. Evidence suggests it was invented by one Hong Kong restaurant, now expanded into a chain. Regardless of its roots, the dish has won wide acceptance. Homes and finer restaurants have added it to their culinary repertoire, and the latter serve it with almost as much pomp and circumstance as a Peking duck.

The idea is to spread a minced filling with sauce on a raw lettuce leaf, roll, and eat.

The filling is customarily minced pigeon meat with chopped bamboo shoots, seasoned with garlic, ginger, wine and soy sauces to give it red colour. Minced pork and mushrooms is also known, as is the fact that virtually any minced pork, beef, chicken, fish or shellfish filling, with or without chopped vegetables such as bamboo shoots, winter mushrooms, onions etc., will do. Remember to use richly flavoured ingredients, to chop them finely, and to cook the sauce well into the ingredients, or thicken it, in order to make it manageable for rolling and eating. Serve small dishes of sauces—such as chilli sauce, hoi sin sauce, plum sauce etc.—to spread with the filling.

A second version of this "saang choi bau," 生菜包 (literally: lettuce-wrapping) is as a variation of the Cantonese Hot-pot or Da Been Lo, as described on p. 43. Customarily, head lettuce is used to wrap the minced pigeon filling, while leaf lettuce is used to wrap the hot-pot filling.

WHITE WORMWOOD
Junn jiu choi 珍珠菜

APPEARANCE: Distinguish this vegetable by the 8–10″ long reddish-purple leaf stalks and sparse, trifoliate leaf blades.

QUALITY: Select well-formed leaves which appear freshly picked.

GENERAL COMMENTS: These leaves have a strong, rather resinous or "floral" taste remotely similar to chrysanthemum leaves. In fact, they come from plants of the same botanical family as chrysanthemum and lettuce, and of the same genus as true wormwood or absinthe.

PREPARATION: Wash and chop, discarding toughest lower portions of leaf stalks.

COOKING: People of Chiu Chow serve this green fried as a side dish; the Cantonese use it to make a tonic soup in the simple style described below. Use it sparingly.

White Wormwood Soup

Lean pork, shredded and seasoned
White wormwood, washed and chopped

Bring water to a boil, add pork and simmer until broth is well flavoured. Add vegetable, using about one cup or less of chopped leaves to four cups of broth. Simmer briefly to cook leaves thoroughly, season with salt and serve.

GARLAND CHRYSANTHEMUM

Tong ho 茼蒿

APPEARANCE: A casual glance might mistake the leafy stalks of chrysanthemum for a Chinese cabbage. Note, however, that chrysanthemum leaves are bluntly lobed, have stalks more like lettuce, and feel slightly rough in texture.

QUALITY: Select plants with unblemished, crisp leaves, preferably without signs of flowering.

GENERAL COMMENTS: For Oriental peoples the chrysanthemum is a plant for all seasons. In spring, gardeners train plants for autumn floral displays; in summer housewives and herbalists brew a cooling tea from dried petals. In the autumn wild blossoms adorn hillsides while their descendants adorn gardens and pose for portraits on silk. In winter the leaves and petals are cooked.

Technically more than one species of chrysanthemum serves these many purposes. Wild chrysanthemums are distinct from the cultivated; of the latter, one species provides myriad varieties of ornamental flowers, while another provides vegetables. Within the edible species three varieties exist: one which the Japanese grow for leaves; one which the Chinese grow for leaves; and one which the Chinese grow for flower petals, mostly used to garnish snake meat dishes.

Chrysanthemum leaves have a subtle but distinct resinous or "floral" flavour which is best enjoyed in small quantities, accompanied by other flavours, and cooked only briefly.

PREPARATION: Separate leaves from central stalk; wash well.

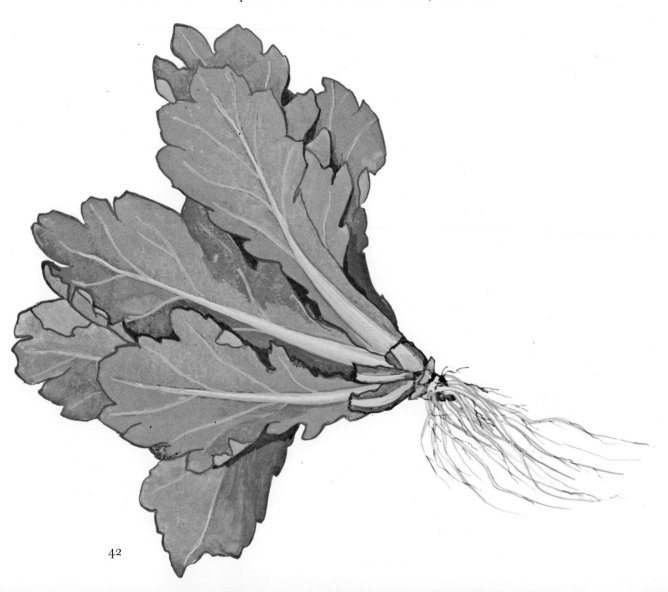

COOKING: Hunan Chinese sometimes stir-fry tong ho as a vegetable on its own; Cantonese generally use it only to make soup. For a quick version of the latter, simply flavour boiling water with shreds of lean pork or chicken (or a stock cube), add the chrysanthemum— either alone or with other suitably mild-flavoured vegetables such as bean curd, lettuce or fresh mushrooms—season with light soy sauce, and serve.

Alternatively you may let your guests cook their own soup, as described below. This soup-fondue is a traditional Cantonese meal enjoyed in restaurants and homes alike, exclusively in the winter when the steaming pot both cooks the food and warms the diners.

Cantonese Hot-pot or Da Been Lo

Equipment: 1 pot of boiling water with heat source strong enough to keep the water simmering throughout the cooking; e.g. a rice cooker, crockpot, charcoal hibachi, pot on portable gas burner, etc.

Cooking implement for each diner: e.g. fondue forks, short skewers, small wire baskets with long handles, wooden chopsticks, etc.

Ingredients: A selection of fresh vegetables, prepared in bite-size pieces, such as:
Bean curd
Lettuce
Peking cabbage
Bean sprouts
Chrysanthemum leaves, etc.
A selection of very fresh meat, sliced as thinly as possible, such as:
Pork
Beef
Liver
Chicken
Squid, etc.
Mungbean vermicelli, soaked, chopped in 4–5″ lengths
Winter mushrooms, soaked
Noodles

Condiments: Small dishes of sauces for dipping, such as light soy sauce, chilli sauce, mustard, custom mixtures, beaten raw egg, etc.

Procedure: Place the pot in the middle of the table; add the mushrooms (best left in the pot until near the end as they help flavour the stock), cover and bring to a boil. Add some of each of the vegetables and vermicelli at this point, and periodically throughout the meal. Cooking the meat proceeds as with a French fondue; that is, each person skewers a morsel, dips it raw into the broth, when cooked into a sauce, and when cool into his mouth. In some households the cooked morsels are dipped into raw beaten egg, then wrapped in a raw lettuce leaf and eaten as "saang choi bau."

When cooking has finished, add the noodles to the pot of broth. Finally serve each diner with a bowl of noodles and an exquisitely flavoured soup to end the meal.

LONG BEANS
Dau gok 豆角

APPEARANCE: "Long" aptly describes these beans because they measure literally 1–3 feet in length. There are two colours to choose from: light green, known as "baak dau gok" or 白豆角; and dark green, known as "tseng dau gok" or 青豆角.

QUALITY: The light coloured beans are considered flabby, while the darker ones are considered to be more tasty, firm and tender. As with string beans, the smaller the swellings (i.e. the bean seeds inside the pod), the better the pods.

GENERAL COMMENTS: Botanically, these beans belong to a different genus than string beans, but the same genus and species as cowpeas or black-eyed peas. Historically, they have been growing in China since before recorded time. Patient, northern Chinese grow them to maturity for the dry peas, while the southerners prefer to cook the immature pods.

In taste, long beans are hardly distinguishable from string beans; however, textures differ significantly. Because these pods are so narrow, they are less succulent but more crunchy, and cook faster.

PREPARATION: Wash; chop into 1″ lengths for Chinese dishes, or as desired—no strings attached.

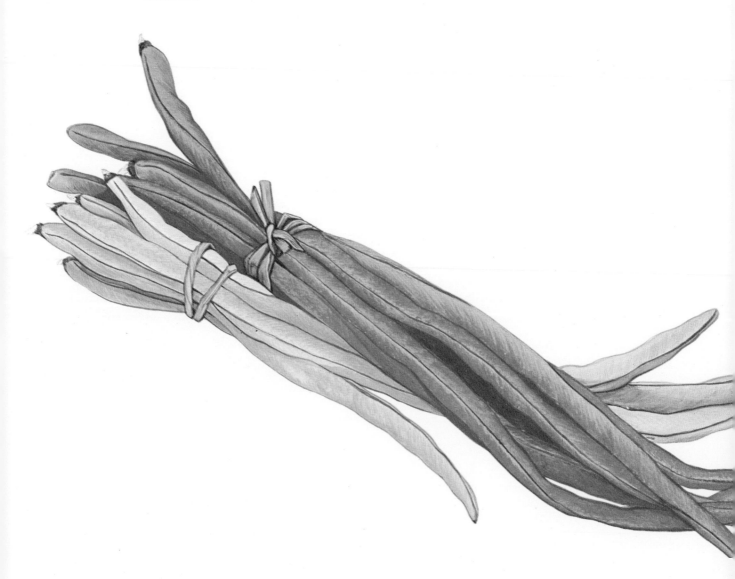

COOKING: Long beans may be unequivocally substituted for French green beans, and vice versa. The Cantonese commonly enjoy these; and commonly cook them in one of the following three ways. First, they may be stir-fried in Chinese omelettes as described for mungbean sprouts (p. 48). In this case, add the eggs to them alone, or with shredded meat and/or other vegetables. Secondly, long beans are particularly good prepared in a black bean sauce with pork of some sort (shreds of meat; ribs; stomach etc.). Thirdly, they are amenable to being stir-fried at random with whatever else happens to be available, as in the following:

Vegetable Medley

Peanuts
Long beans, chopped in 1″ lengths
Celery, sliced thinly on the diagonal
Shrimp, cleaned and rubbed with a little salt
Spring onions, chopped in 1″ lengths

Heat oil; fry peanuts until golden; remove and drain. Remove excess oil from wok, leaving just enough for the vegetables. When oil is quite hot, stir-fry beans and celery, seasoning them with salt and a pinch of sugar; remove from wok when just tender. Again heat oil; stir-fry shrimps quickly, return vegetables, peanuts and spring onions. Toss, season with a dash of soy sauce, and serve.

SUGAR PEAS, SNOW PEAS OR EDIBLE PEAPODS

Hoh laan dau 荷蘭豆

APPEARANCE: Distinguishing sugar peas from shell peas is a matter of bulge. Edible peapods are flat, with small, discrete and prominent bulges corresponding to the immature peas inside. Shell peas, on the other hand, have uniformly and fully inflated pods with large peas inside. Plant breeders annually develop new varieties which differ in size (2–4″ in length), sweetness and tenderness.

QUALITY: Within any single variety, the smaller the pod and the smaller the peas inside the pod, the more tender and sweet the peapods.

GENERAL COMMENTS: The belief that edible peapods are a quintessential and traditional Oriental food seems to be an illusion. The Cantonese name "hoh laan," a corruption of "Holland," may more accurately indicate this vegetable's origins. The garden pea species first appeared in southwestern Asia, whence it spread east to China, arriving during the T'ang Dynasty, 7th century A.D., and west to Europe. The Chinese seem to have preferred their own peas and beans, while Europeans greeted this new one with great appetite. In those early days only the dried ripe seeds were eaten; during the 16th century immature peas became a delicacy; and within the last century this trend of earlier and earlier harvesting seems to have culminated in the harvest of the very pods themselves.

Like green beans, all peapods are edible, but the varieties grown for the purpose are more delectable because they lack a certain parchment-like layer lining and toughening of the pod. In any case, peapods are crisp in texture, verdant and sweet. Smaller varieties are often more choice to eat but more tedious to prepare.

PREPARATION: Strings running lengthwise on both edges of the pod must be removed. Accomplish this efficiently by snapping the stem end off, leaving one string attached, tearing that string off top to bottom, then grasping and tearing the other string off bottom to top.

COOKING:

Western. Nibble raw. Parboil or steam, and serve salted, peppered and buttered. Sauté lightly with a sprig of mint, thyme or basil.

Chinese. The Cantonese stir-fry this vegetable alone with crushed bits of ginger and garlic, or with other vegetables (particularly mungbean sprouts) and/or with shreds of pork, beef, chicken or liver.

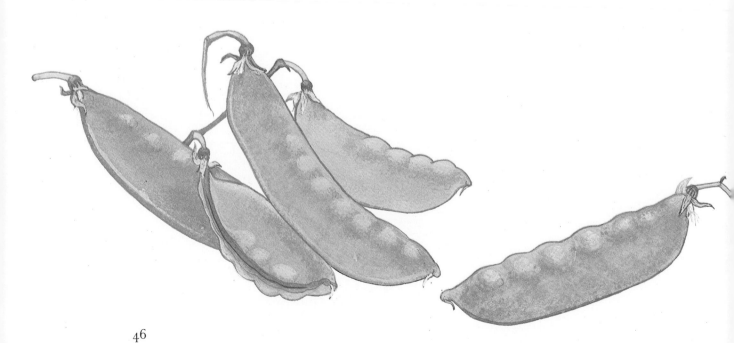

MUNGBEAN SPROUTS

Sai dau nga choi 細豆芽菜
Nga choi jai 芽菜仔
Silver Sprouts: Ngunn nga choi 銀芽菜

APPEARANCE: "Sai" means small; "dau" are beans; "nga" means bud, and "choi" is vegetable. The subsequent deduction that these are the sprouting buds of little beans is accurate.

In Hong Kong, only two sorts of bean sprouts are sold: mungbean and soybean (or "big bean") sprouts. They are perennially available in markets, and markets are within walking distance of everyone, so no one sprouts beans themselves. Sprout vendors often have two jumbled heaps of mungbean sprouts: one of sprouts with the $\frac{1}{4}$"-long green-skinned bean still attached; and one of pure shoots, bereft of both heads and tails. The latter is called "ngunn nga choi," or silver sprouts, and costs more due to the labour of berefting them.

QUALITY: Bean sprouts should be clean, clear and white from head to tail, with only a hint of leaves emerging from the bean. Short fat sprouts are more tender than long or greenish ones.

GENERAL COMMENTS: Bean sprouts are more nutritious and delicious than beans because sprouting transforms starch into vitamins, sugars and tender young plant. Silver sprouts, like bread without the crust, are considered finer than whole nga choi. They cook slightly more evenly and quickly, and look more uniform when served. Thus, restaurants always serve them; they are preferred for filling spring rolls*; but ordinary housewives seldom consider them worth the extra price.

In preparing mungbean sprouts remember that they are mostly water. This means that their taste is mild, as they cook they shrink, and that water released during shrinking will thin the sauce. Mungbean sprouts may be eaten raw or cooked. If the latter, do it quickly over high heat.

When storing sprouts, preserve their lily white translucence by keeping them in water, in a covered container, in the fridge. Nga choi will keep at least two days this way; ngunn nga choi must be used more quickly.

*A Cantonese spring roll, "chun goon" 春卷, is a savoury mixture of meat and vegetables wrapped in pastry and deep-fried. This is distinct from an egg roll which, for people of Hong Kong and Macau, is a sweet, made from egg and flour batter, similar in taste and crisp texture to the American "Chinese fortune cookie."

PREPARATION: If time allows, remove unsightly tails; if ceremony dictates, remove both heads and tails. Wash and drain. Do not bother to remove the green seed coats of the beans because they are harmlessly, tastelessly edible.

COOKING:

Western. Toss in salads raw, or blanch and marinate. For a vegetable side dish, sauté or blanch in chicken stock, toss with butter, minced scallions and/or herbs, and serve.

Chinese. This versatile veg is stir-fried alone, with meat, poultry, fish, seafood, or simply with other vegetables. The Cantonese most commonly stir-fry it with shredded pork, with spring onion and shreds of meat in omelettes, or in fried noodle dishes where the mouth discerns it but not the eye.

Chinese Omelette

1 tablespoon ham, cut in slivers
2–3 cups mungbean sprouts
2 small eggs, lightly beaten and seasoned with salt and pepper

In hot oil in wok, over high heat, fry ham lightly and immediately add sprouts; stir and toss. When sprouts are shiny, wilting and almost cooked, pour eggs over and stir. When, a few seconds later, the eggs set, remove to serving dish and serve.

Prepared properly, this dish is mainly crisp sprouts, lightly bound together by a soft, lightly ham-flavoured egg custard. You may add minced spring onions and slivers of cooked carrot for colour; and of course you may substitute any other meat, poultry, shrimps etc., for the ham.

Loong Suk's Village Noodles

Broad white rice noodles (hoh fun 河粉), fresh; or broad egg noodles, cooked and drained
Mungbean sprouts
Dried shrimp, soaked
Fresh fish meat
Peanuts, fried or roasted
Sesame seeds, roasted

Mince both shrimp meat and fish; combine, season with salt and white pepper. Heat oil in wok, season with a crushed slice of fresh ginger, then fry fish; remove. Heat oil again, over high heat, stir-fry sprouts and remove. Finally, fry noodles, add all ingredients, stir and toss, season with soy sauce and serve.

Bok Bang

Another popular use of mungbean sprouts is as a filling for Peking pancakes or tortillas (bok bang 薄餅) as described below. These pancakes make a good educational meal for people who think Chinese food always means rice.

Ingredients: All-purpose white wheat flour: 1 cup will make 4–6 pancakes, depending on size; figure $\frac{2}{3}$–1 cup flour per person.
Hot water, approximately half as much water as flour
Oil

Method: Measure flour into large bowl. Add water while stirring until a cohesive ball of dough forms. Turn dough out onto counter and knead, dusting hands and counter with flour as needed to prevent sticking. When dough has become smooth and elastic (after about 10 minutes), let it rest 20–60 minutes, either on the counter or in a bowl, covered.

When ready, heat a dry fry-pan over medium heat. Pinch off two 1″-diameter balls of dough. Roll each into a smooth ball, then flatten into a 2″ diameter circle. Brush one surface of one circle lightly with oil, press other circle onto it, then roll this sandwich to a circle 7–8″ in diameter. Transfer to hot fry-pan. After several minutes, flip; cook until both sides have golden brown spots. Remove from pan, peel the two tortillas apart, avoiding steam burns if possible, and stack one on top of the other, wet side to dry side. Continue with remaining dough.

The bok bang may be prepared one day in advance, refrigerated, then rewarmed to a pliable state by baking or steaming them wrapped in aluminium foil.

Filling: Pork, shredded and seasoned
Mungbean sprouts
Mungbean vermicelli, soaked
Jew's ear mushrooms, soaked
(Bamboo shoots, chopped in strips)
(Chinese cabbage, either baak choi or wong nga baak, chopped in strips)
2 eggs

In hot oil in wok, cook a smashed slice of ginger until fragrant, remove and discard. Fry pork; remove. Heat oil again until very hot, add sprouts, stir and toss until beginning to shrink, then add mushrooms, bamboo shoots and cabbage. When almost cooked, return pork with vermicelli. Season liberally with light soy sauce; toss and cook to blend flavours. Excess liquid should either boil away or be absorbed by the vermicelli; if, after 2–3 minutes liquid still remains, thicken it into a sauce with cornstarch. Remove to a serving dish.

To make the egg topping, like the upper shell of a turtle: Beat eggs lightly and season with salt and pepper. Pour eggs into lightly greased wok or small fry-pan in a thin stream, making a circle the size of the serving dish. Tilt pan for even distribution and cooking. When cooked, place on top of vegetables, and serve.

Condiments: Prepare small bowls of the following:
Thin slices, 2–3″ long, of leek or spring onion
Thin, equally long, sticks of cucumber
Hoi sin sauce (海鮮醬), thinned with hot water to a spreading consistency

Method of Eating: Each person prepares his own dinner by spreading a little hoi sin sauce on a pancake, adding condiments and filling to taste, and then rolling it up, folding in the sides in the hope of preventing juices from leaking out. The host must be sure to supply tissues, napkins or hand-towels for messy fingers.

Variations: It should be noted that this filling may be served instead as an accompaniment for rice. Likewise, other mixtures and other condiments may be used to fill the pancakes. Let your imagination loose, bounded only by the general observation that fillings made up of small, boneless bits and little or thick sauce are most convenient.

SOYBEAN SPROUTS
Daai dau nga choi 大豆芽菜

APPEARANCE: "Nga choi" are bean sprouts; "daai dau" means big beans and thus, not coincidentally, shoppers readily identify these sprouts by the large seed attached. Soybean sprouts measure 2–3″ in length and have a yellow, $\frac{1}{2}$″ long bean at one end. Whereas mungbean sprouts are often displayed in jumbled heaps, these are usually neatly aligned, either tied in bunches or arranged in a circle, heads to the outside and root-tails in, like a many-spoked wheel.

QUALITY: The beans should be yellow with no tint of green or hint of emerging leaves; the shoot should be clear, crisp and white from head to tip.
(N.B. Green soybean sprouts are not harmful to eat, just less delicious.)

GENERAL COMMENTS: Soybean sprouts are one of the most nutritious and economical foods available. Unlike other vegetables, soybeans have high levels of protein and oils which make them comparable in food value to meat and eggs, and which give them a rich, nutty taste. The process of sprouting converts much of their already minimal starch into vitamins (particularly vitamin C), enzymes, and tender, sweet new plant.

Cooks should keep three precautions in mind when preparing this vegetable: First, because raw soybeans are slightly poisonous, these sprouts must always be cooked before eating. Second, soy sprouts are less tender than mungbean sprouts and will be even more fibrous if old or overcooked. Third, sprouts will keep longer and remain whiter if stored in water in a covered container in the fridge.

PREPARATION: Align the sprouts in a bunch on a chopping board and trim off the lower, root portions with a single blow of a cleaver. Then wash and drain, discarding any blackened or otherwise disreputable heads.

COOKING:
Western. Blanch in boiling salted water, drain, and marinate with other vegetables (chopped tomatoes, celery, green pepper, fuzzy melon, spring onions, etc.) in an oil and vinegar dressing. Saute. Or, mince and combine with minced beef to make meat loaf, stuffing for green peppers or cabbage leaves, hamburger patties, casseroles, etc. Minced finely, the shoots blend into such mixtures undetectably, while chopped coarsely the beans add a welcome dimension of crunch.
Chinese. Three styles of preparation of this vegetable seem standard among the Cantonese: simply stir-fried with ginger (and pork, optional); boiled with pork bones to make a traditional "poor man's" soup stock; and minced with pork in a meat patty.

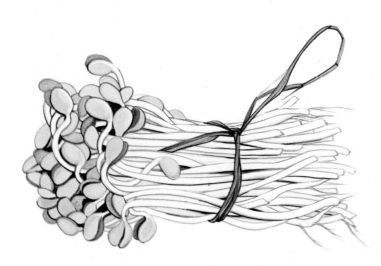

Pork & Soy Sprout Soup

Pork bones or meat
Soybean sprouts
1–2 slices of fresh ginger, crushed

Combine all ingredients and boil until broth is well-flavoured—several hours for bones, less for meat. Interestingly enough, even after long boiling, the beans will remain whole and not disintegrate as lentils and split peas do. Thus the final soup is a broth and not a porridge.

Pork & Soybean Mince

½ lb. lean pork, minced, seasoned
½–1 lb. soybean sprouts, minced
(1–2 winter mushrooms, soaked, chopped)
(1–2 tsp. dried shrimp, soaked, chopped)
1 slice of fresh ginger, crushed

In hot oil, fry a crushed slice of ginger until fragrant; discard. If using shrimp, fry them now, then add sprouts and mushrooms. Toss and continue cooking over medium heat 3–4 minutes until done; remove. Reheat oil, fry meat, return vegetables, stir and toss. Adjust seasoning with soy sauce and, when flavours are thoroughly blended, dish and serve.

BEAN CURD
Dau foo 豆腐

Like other vegetables, bean curd has evolved into varieties, of which four will be described on the following pages.

Fresh bean curd (alias "dau foo," "dofu" or "tofu") is produced from the water extract of yellow soybeans. The beans are first soaked, then pulverized in water; solids are filtered out and the remaining liquid suspension is cooked briefly to detoxify soybeans' harmful chemicals. Finally powdered calcium carbonate (or an aluminium compound) is added to cause the suspension to curdle. Fresh curd may be sold as is or processed by pressing, frying, drying or fermenting.

Nutritionally, dau foo has the water-soluble vitamins, minerals and protein of soybeans without the starch. This sounds good and builds strong bodies, but tastes bland. Bean curd in any state—except fermented!—has little flavour; varieties of fresh dau foo differ mainly in texture, which is what determines the different methods of cooking used for each.

WATER BEAN CURD
Seui dau foo 水豆腐

This is the most common, and perhaps the most versatile, type of bean curd. Traditionally, it is made in cloth-lined wooden trays about 12″ square which are stacked as the curd is made and gradually unstacked as the curd is sold. Machine-made bean curd is sold packaged in plastic boxes.

Fresh seui dau foo should be shiny, white, smooth on all surfaces, with a faint, clean fragrance of soybeans. Because of its delicate texture it is best used for steaming, braising or simmering briefly in soup where it is least likely to disintegrate under rough handling. Use this to make "Lo Siu Ping On" as described for Wrapped Bean Curd, or any of the following.

Green & Bean Curd Soup

Bring water to the boil; flavour it with seasoned sliced lean pork, fish meat, fish balls or a chicken stock cube. Adjust seasoning with light soy sauce, white pepper and cooked oil. Carefully add squares of bean curd, and tuck lettuce or other leafy vegetable in around the edges. Simmer 4–5 minutes, and serve.

Stuffed Bean Curd

Bean curd
Stuffing: Seasoned minced pork; or seasoned minced beef; or fresh shrimp paste as described below
Sauce: Light soy sauce, white pepper, sesame oil, cornstarch

Making shrimp paste: Clean the shrimp. Mash—do not chop—them, either with a spoon and a bowl, with a rolling pin and a plastic bag, or with the broadside of a cleaver crushing them on a chopping board. Scrape the paste into a bowl, season with salt, white pepper, cornstarch and—if desirable and available—dashes of wine, sesame oil and ginger juice. To combine and give the paste a smooth texture, stir it vigorously with a chopstick or fork, in one direction only, for several minutes.

Stuffing the bean curd: This may be done in any of a variety of ways. (1) Cut each block of curd in half diagonally; cut a slit in the diagonal face, sprinkle with corn-starch, and stuff in a dab of filling. (2) Slice the curd in half horizontally, dust cut surfaces with cornstarch, spread with filling and replace lid, as in making sandwiches or a layer cake. (3) Dust the top of the curd with cornstarch and spread with filling.

Cooking: Either: (1) Steam the pieces on a shallow dish until filling is cooked; finally garnish with chopped spring onions, dribble with light soy sauce and drizzle with hot cooked oil. Or: (2) Braise the pieces in chicken stock in a saucepan; finally remove them to serving dish and dress with the braising sauce seasoned with soy sauce and thickened with cornstarch.

Braised Bean Curd

Pork, shredded, seasoned
Garlic, crushed
1–2 slices fresh ginger, crushed
Bean curd, whole or in quarters or eighths
Any or all of the following:
    Winter mushrooms, soaked
    Fresh mushrooms
    Bamboo shoots, sliced
    Shallots or spring onions, chopped

In a casserole or saucepan, lightly fry pork with garlic and ginger. Add bean curd and brown lightly on all sides. Add other vegetables, soy sauce and light stock or water. Cover and braise 10–20 minutes. Adjust seasoning with dashes of sesame oil, white pepper and soy sauce. Serve as is or, if sauce seems thin, remove solid ingredients to the serving dish, thicken remaining liquid with cornstarch, pour over rest and then serve.

For variety, you may modify the above directions slightly and subsequently produce a spicier Shanghai dish known as "Ma Poh Dau Foo" 麻婆豆腐. The modifications are as follows: Mince the pork; mash the bean curd; add no other vegetables; use approximately 1 part by volume of pork per 1–2 parts bean curd, and season two cups of mixture with 1–2 tablespoons chilli-bean paste ("dau baan laat jeung" 豆板辣醬). At a pinch, you may substitute minced fresh chillies with salted yellow beans ("meen see" 麵豉) or fermented black beans, mashed, for the chilli-bean paste.

WRAPPED BEAN CURD
Bo baau dau foo 布包豆腐

This bean curd is sold from tubs of water rather than from a wooden board or plastic box. Each square has been wrapped in cloth, so pieces have rounded edges and cost 2–3 times more than common fresh dau foo. This is the finest, most delicate curd, and is usually used only for steaming as in the following traditional Cantonese dish:

Lo Siu Ping On 老少平安

3 squares bean curd (bo baau or seui type)
2–3 oz. very fresh fish meat, minced
2 oz. lean pork, minced
1–2 spring onions, minced

Combine pork and fish; season with salt, white pepper, a dash of sugar, light soy sauce, cornstarch, 1–2 drops of sesame oil and a little cooked oil. Mash bean curd with a fork in a dish, add seasoned meats, then mash all together until homogenous. Spread mixture in a shallow dish or enamelled pan, sprinkle with spring onions and steam above boiling water (or cooking rice) 10–15 minutes or until pork is cooked. If desired, top with more light soy sauce (or half light-half dark soy sauces) and cooked oil just before serving.

DRY OR PRESSED BEAN CURD
Dau foo gonn 豆腐乾

This type of curd is solid, and thus easily sliced or cut in shreds and stir-fried. Two types exist, as illustrated: the larger, 3″ square white one is plain; the smaller, 2″ square reddish one is lightly coated with 5-spice powder (ng heung fun 五香粉). Both tend to be bland in taste and dry in texture, so prepare them with a rich sauce or with other highly flavoured, slightly oily ingredients. Matchstick shreds of dau foo gonn may be included in Chinese omelettes, as described for mungbean sprouts, p. 48, or in Shanghai dishes with pork and chilli-bean sauce. Small cubes of it may be included in mixed stir-fry dishes as described below:

54

Chau Ngup-ngup

3 squares dau foo gonn
$\frac{1}{2}$–1 cup green peas
$\frac{1}{4}$–$\frac{1}{2}$ cup pickled Chinese radish (choi po 菜譜)
Carrot, cooked
Chilli pepper
Green pepper
Lean pork meat

Rinse pickled radish well to remove excess salt. Chop all ingredients into $\frac{1}{4}''$ cubes. Heat oil in wok; fry pickled radish, then add other vegetables except bean curd. Stir and toss until cooked; remove. Reheat oil; fry meat and bean curd simultaneously. Return vegetables; season with soy sauce, dashes of sugar and white pepper while continuing to stir and toss. When flavours have blended, dish and serve.

DEEP-FRIED BEAN CURD
Dau foo pok 豆腐泡

These are small cubes or squares of bean curd which have been, quite simply, deep-fried. The outer surface is crusty and golden-yellow in colour, while the inside is porous. Usually, dau foo pok are braised, either au naturel or with a minced pork or fish stuffing.

Produce dau foo pok yourself by deep-frying small cubes of fresh bean curd. Otherwise, if you buy them, remove excess oil and tenacious dirt by parboiling or pouring boiling water over them. Then try the following:

Mushrooms & Dau Foo Pok with Lettuce

Lettuce
Dau foo pok
Mushrooms, either dried and soaked, or fresh
Oyster sauce

Parboil or stir-fry lettuce and mound on serving dish. In hot oil, fry a crushed slice of ginger until fragrant, then add mushrooms and pieces of dau foo pok. Toss and cook 1 minute, then add a little water or light stock, oyster sauce and light soy sauce, cover and simmer several minutes. Uncover, adjust seasoning, thicken sauce with cornstarch and pour over lettuce.

WINTER MELON
Dong gwa 冬瓜

APPEARANCE: This is one of the largest vegetables grown. Mature winter melons resemble their cousins, watermelons, in shape but outstrip them in size (10″ or more in diameter) and in weight (up to 100 lbs.). The dark green skin is thin, hard and waxy—giving them their other common name, "wax gourd."

In the market expect to see only part of a whole melon because it is commonly sold by the slice.

QUALITY: Buy slices which have been freshly cut, with firm, white flesh which smells clean.

GENERAL COMMENTS: Winter melon has nourished Asians since earliest times. This has required a lot of melon because 96–97% of it is water. Diners particularly welcome its juicy flesh during hot weather, but cooks must have strong spirit lest that flesh be weak. For best results when cooking winter melon, remember to offset its blandness with generous seasoning; expect it to release considerable liquid as it cooks; and eat soon after purchase because the cut surfaces will deteriorate and send off-flavours through the porous flesh quickly.

PREPARATION: Remove seeds and coarse fibres at centre of melon. Peel; rinse. Chop in chunks for boiling, in matchstick or fan-shaped slices for stir-frying; or as desired.

COOKING:

Western. Like any summer squash (or like Chinese fuzzy melon), winter melon may be sauted, steamed, braised or baked. The result, however, tends to be watery, tasteless and translucent. Deal with these deficiencies either by compensating for them with seasoning; ignoring them; or avoiding them altogether by making soup as the Chinese do.

Chinese. Although winter melon may be stir-fried in any of the ways described for fuzzy melon—with compensation for its weaker taste and more spongy texture—the Cantonese prefer to make soup with it. During summer, traditional and motherly cooks boil dong gwa with barley, lablab beans, dried kapok flowers, lotus seed pods and other herbs to make a tonic drink. The most elaborate and famous dinner dish made with this vegetable is Winter Melon Pond (Dong Gwa Jong 冬瓜盅). This soup is cooked and served in a whole melon whose skin has been decoratively carved with auspicious motifs such as dragons and phoenixes.

As Winter Melon Pond is beyond the cooking (but not eating!) capacities of most Chinese families, winter melon usually goes into soup, rather than vice versa. To make melon soup, boil water together with any of the following ingredients as long as necessary to get a good broth; then add the melon during the last half hour of simmering.

> Suggested stock bases:
> Pork, meat or bones, and winter mushrooms;
> Barbecued duck (siu ngop 燒鴨), meat and bones;
> Dried shrimp (soaked; fried lightly in oil with fresh ginger first) and mungbean vermicelli (soaked);
> Ham shreds and fresh mushrooms;
> Chicken, meat or bones;
> Salted egg (haam daan 咸蛋); etc.

N.B. For a miniature version of Winter Melon Pond see recipe with bottle gourd, p. 61.

FUZZY MELON
Tseet gwa 節瓜

APPEARANCE: Subtle dumbbell shape, faint covering of white hairs and slightly blotchy colouring distinguish this melon. Larger than a cucumber, it usually measures 6–10″ long, $1\frac{1}{2}$–2″ in diameter.

QUALITY: Select small solid green ones; the younger they are the firmer the flesh.

GENERAL COMMENTS: Fuzzy melons are a race of winter melon. These are harvested while still young so the flesh, while generally bland, has slightly more flavour and a distinctly firmer texture than winter melon.

PREPARATION: Wash; scrub to remove the hairs or peel. For stir-frying, chop in match-sticks, $\frac{1}{4}$″ diameter and 2″ long, or in semi-circles, $\frac{1}{4}$″ thick.

COOKING:

Western. Fuzzy melon is a Chinese version of summer squash. Like courgettes and zucchini, it may be steamed, boiled, braised, sautéd, baked, pickled or simply eaten raw. Take advantage of its bland but sponge-like character by seasoning it liberally and richly, with herbs, cheese, nuts, sesame seeds, or meat en casserole. Purée it for soup; cream it au gratin; stuff it with any minced meat and/or vegetable filling. Imagination and applied experience are the most important ingredients in preparing this vegetable tastefully.

Chinese. This vegetable is a Cantonese favourite, abundant in the markets and versatile in the kitchen. It may be steamed, braised, boiled or stir-fried—with chicken, beef, pork, fish and/or other vegetables and/or dried foods. Consider it a good sponge for absorbing, blending and enhancing other flavours, but always remember to provide those other flavours for it to work on. If you stir-fry it alone, add a chicken stock cube; otherwise stir-fry it with chicken and walnuts; with shrimp; with beef and oyster sauce; or with its most traditional wok-mates, pork and mushrooms.

58

Fun See & Fuzzy Melon Soup

Lean pork, thinly sliced and seasoned
1 fuzzy melon, peeled and chopped coarsely
1 Chinese salted egg (haam daan 咸蛋)
2–4 winter mushrooms (dong gwoo 冬菇), soaked
1 handful mungbean vermicelli (fun see 粉絲), soaked

Bring 5–6 cups of water with pork, winter mushrooms and mushroom soaking liquid to a boil. Simmer until broth is well flavoured, about 30 minutes. Cut vermicelli into shorter, more manageable (i.e. 4–5″) lengths, then add to broth. Meanwhile, rinse black powder off the egg and crack the latter directly into the soup while stirring vigorously to break the egg white into fine shreds. Continue to simmer the soup 10 minutes or so. Adjust seasoning with soy sauce if necessary, and serve.

Melon, Mushroom & Pork

Lean pork, sliced in shreds and seasoned
Winter mushrooms, soaked
Fuzzy melon
(Dried shrimps, (1 teaspoon per $\frac{1}{2}$ cup pork) soaked)
(Spring onions or shallots)
1–2 slices fresh ginger, crushed

This combination of ingredients may be prepared in any of the following ways:
  (1) Stir-fried. In this case you may use winter mushrooms, jew's ear mushrooms or fresh mushrooms; you may add onions; you may substitute any of the melons (or winter squash) for the fuzzy; omit the shrimp. Stir-fry the melon and mushrooms (with ginger) first; remove; then stir-fry the pork (with garlic), return the veg, season with soy sauce, thicken sauce with a little cornstarch to help flavours stick to the melon, and serve.
  (2) Boiled. Use pork meat or bones; you may substitute any of the melons except angled luffa. Fry the shrimps with ginger in a little oil first, then add water and the remaining ingredients and boil until broth is flavoured.
  (3) Steamed or braised. Wash and peel melon; cut in half lengthwise. Cut mushrooms in thin shreds. Place melons on steaming dish, cut sides up; cover with a single layer of mushroom and pork shreds. Steam or braise lightly until pork is done and melon is tender. Make a sauce with mushroom-soaking liquid or chicken stock or braising liquid with soy sauce, a pinch of sugar and cornstarch; pour this over the steamed melon and serve.
  (4) Stuffed. Mince pork, onions, mushrooms and shrimps together; season with salt, white pepper, soy sauce, sugar and cornstarch; blend well. To prepare melon, cut it in half crosswise and scoop out seeds with a long-handled spoon. Dust inner surface lightly with cornstarch to help the stuffing adhere. Stuff with minced pork mixture.
    In saucepan lightly fry ginger with melons: first on the cut ends, then briefly on their sides. Add a little water or chicken stock, cover and braise until tender, 15–30 minutes. Occasionally turn the melons so they cook evenly and add water as necessary to prevent burning.
    When done, remove melons to serving dish and slice into $\frac{1}{2}$″, bite-size rounds. Season the liquid remaining in the pan, thicken with cornstarch into a sauce which you can then pour over the melon slices. Serve.

BOTTLE GOURD

APPEARANCE: The bottle gourd species embraces a spectrum of variation in shape and size. The two examples given here both have the smooth tough skin and light green colour characteristic of the species.

Bottleneck Gourd (葫蘆瓜) Woo lo gwa: Identify this gourd by its beautiful figure.

Hairy Gourd (蒲瓜) Po gwa: This melon resembles a baseball bat. Its shape may be straight or curved; its skin is usually sparsely hairy; the size is generally large (12–30″ long).

QUALITY: Young gourds are tender; older ones become tough; and mature ones develop knife-defying solidarity. (Fortunately this last type seldom reaches market as farmers keep it for making bottles.) Choose small, tender gourds without sign of rot or worms.

GENERAL COMMENTS: Tighter than a sealed drum, more durable than a plastic bag, cheaper than tupperware, this gourd is believed to have floated from Africa, its native home, to South America, where it was growing by 7000–5000 B.C. Later varieties, perhaps less seaworthy, eventually reached Asia, where they have been grown, dried and used as receptacles ever since.

In China, the woo lo gwa is legendary. Ancient artwork inevitably portrays sages and monks with one or two of these gourds dangling from their belts, transporting water or herbs. The term "woo lo" (葫蘆) has no other meaning than to describe the shape of this particular vegetable.

Gastronomically, these gourds have the same basic attributes of other Chinese summer melons (fuzzy melon, winter melon, etc.). The flesh is firm and white, with an exceptionally fine-grained texture and mild taste.

N.B. To make bottles, the gourds must be harvested when dead ripe; they are then hollowed out and dried, preferably over heat, such as an open fire. The shape of the growing gourds may be changed with string, although the shape of the woo lo variety is natural.

PREPARATION: To use woo lo gwa whole as a receptacle for soup or stuffing, slice gourd open at the neck. Remove seeds, scrape the inside lightly, and proceed according to recipe.

For other uses, halve gourd with a sharp knife. Remove seeds, scrape lightly, chop in manageable chunks, peel and slice as desired.

COOKING:

Western. Prepare as you would summer squashes. For novelty, bake the woo lo variety whole with a filling of seasoned minced meats, vegetables and rice as a meal in itself.

Chinese. This melon, particularly the bottleneck version, is more common in ancient legends and paintings than on contemporary dinner tables. It may be boiled in soup or stir-fried in any of the ways described for fuzzy melons.

In addition, the hard skin, bowl shape and diminutive size of the woo lo gwa make it an ideal receptacle for soup cooked in the style of Winter Melon Pond as follows:

Woo Lo Gwa Jong

Ingredients: 1 bottle gourd
Any or all of the following in quantities to taste:
Meat, cooked and thinly sliced: chicken, pork, ham, dried duck, etc.
Winter mushrooms, soaked, whole or sliced
Straw mushrooms
Bamboo shoots
Spring onions
Lotus seeds (leen tzee 蓮子)
Shrimp, fresh or dried, soaked
Chicken stock or water

Equipment: Pot larger than the gourd, with lid
Heatproof dish with sloping sides to support gourd inside the pot
Small dish to cover top of gourd

Method: Slice gourd open at the bottleneck. Scoop out the seeds and spongy flesh of the central cavity, leaving at least 1–2″ of melon towards the outside.

Place melon on supporting dish inside the pot; the rim of the dish must not cut into the melon or the latter will collapse as it softens during cooking. Put ingredients into melon with chicken stock or water to fill approximately $\frac{2}{3}$ full; cover top of gourd with small dish. Add boiling water to just below the lip of the supporting dish; cover pot with its lid. Bring to a boil and simmer gently until melon is cooked, 1–2 hours later. Check occasionally, and replenish water as necessary. The melon is cooked when its flesh is soft and transparent; avoid overcooking otherwise the whole thing will disintegrate.

When done, adjust soup's flavour with salt and white pepper. Serve soup either directly from the gourd, scraping melon from the sides as you dole out the broth, or from a tureen, pouring soup in first and then scraping melon out.

CUCUMBER
Tseng gwa 青瓜

APPEARANCE: Distinguish cucumbers from other melons by their smooth skin and narrow cylindrical shape, usually 1–2″ in diameter. Faint yellow stripes usually radiate from the stem end, and blunt spines may dot the surface.

QUALITY: Choose heavy, firm, small, green ones. Cucumbers become large and yellow as they ripen, which means the spongy seed cavity develops at the expense of the crisp, tastier outer flesh.

GENERAL COMMENTS: By the 6th century A.D. Egyptians, Greeks, Romans and Chinese were cultivating this vegetable, although perhaps not enjoying it as much as modern people because the original varieties were undoubtedly bitter. Today, Westerners know this vegetable as salad or pickle, while Cantonese know it as simply another member of the melon family.

Cucumbers have a firm, crisp and succulent texture with a taste which is distinct, "cool," and rather stronger than the other Chinese melons. Their stems and skin, however, contain chemicals which can be bitter and bitterly indigestible. Peeling removes much of the problem, and salting the chopped or sliced flesh will draw off the rest. This latter process slightly changes the vegetable's texture and seems to help it absorb other flavors (i.e., dressing, sauce, etc.)

PREPARATION: Wash. Peel or score the skin for decorative effect; slice in rounds for salad or cut in rectangular sticks for stir-frying. To remove excess liquid and slight bitterness, mix with a light sprinkling of salt, let stand 10–15 minutes, rinse, drain and squeeze.

COOKING:

Western. Most cucumbers in America and Europe are consumed as pickles: sweet pickles, dill pickles, gherkins, relish, piccalilli etc. Raw cucumbers are sliced in salad or marinated with other veg. Indian "raita" combines hot and cold tastes in a refreshing mixture of cucumber, yoghurt, chilli and chopped mint or coriander.

Chinese. Northern Chinese pickle cucumbers or serve them raw as sticks to accompany Peking pancakes (bok bang, see p. 48). Homestyle, Cantonese cooks stir-fry them with pickled pig's feet and black beans, or in any of the combinations described for fuzzy melon.

YELLOW CUCUMBER
Wong gwa 黃瓜

APPEARANCE: "Yellow torpedo" would be a more accurate name for this vegetable. An average individual measures 10–15″ in length, 4–5″ in diameter and 1–2 pounds in weight.

QUALITY: Select heavy, firm melons; as with cucumbers the smaller they are the less developed the seed cavity and the firmer the flesh.

GENERAL COMMENTS: Predictably enough, this melon has the same characteristics of crisp flesh and cool taste as ordinary cucumbers, but less pronounced. For eating raw, cucumbers are better because they are more tender and crisp; for boiling soup the yellow cucumber is preferred because it withstands cooking better and yields a better flavoured broth.

PREPARATION: For eating raw, peel away tough, yellow skin, remove seeds and slice as desired. For use in soup, scrub well, do not peel and chop into chunks.

COOKING:

Western. Substitute yellow cucumbers for green in any recipe. Eat them raw or cooked; in salads or soup; or pickled.

Chinese. In China, most of the crop becomes a sweet pickle known as "cha gwa" 茶瓜, which is used in soup (see p. 13) or in sweet-and-sour sauces. The Cantonese use the raw melon primarily for soup. The entire melon is used, including seeds and skin, and the broth is believed to be particularly beneficial to the body during hot, sunny weather.

Yellow Cucumber Soup

1 yellow cucumber scrubbed well, chopped into chunks (or green cucumber)
1–1½ lbs. pork bones
2–3 dried Chinese jujubes (mut joe 蜜棗)
1 pair dried duck kidneys (gonn ngop sunn 乾鴨腎)

Combine all ingredients in large pot with 2–3 times as much water. Boil at least two hours; season with salt, and serve.

CHAYOTE
Hop jeung gwa 合掌瓜; **Faat sau gwa** 佛手瓜

APPEARANCE: According to the Cantonese names of this vegetable, it resembles the hands with enfolded fingers of a praying Buddha. Identify it by the enlarged "knuckles" at its base. This variety is also characterized by its pear shape, 4–6″ size and smooth, green skin, but other varieties may be round, spiny and dark green in colour.

QUALITY: Small, hard, light-coloured, immature ones will be the most uniform and most tender in texture.

GENERAL COMMENTS: Buddhist monks sometimes grow this vegetable. This is perhaps because of the religious connotations of its shape, perhaps because the plant is perennial, or perhaps because it grows best at high altitudes, which is where Buddhist monks prefer to grow.

    Chayote has firm white flesh and, unlike other melons, a single, hard, central seed. It is edible raw, peel and all. The taste is mild.

PREPARATION: Wash. Halve it as you would an avocado to remove the seed; chop as desired.

COOKING:

Western. Cut into matchstick-shape, and serve with savoury dips; toss in salad; marinate with other vegetables in an oil-vinegar dressing. Cook it as you would any summer squash.

Chinese. The Cantonese recommend boiling chayote in soup with pork meat or pork bones. It is also amenable to being stir-fried with meat or braised with other tasty ingredients as described for fuzzy melon.

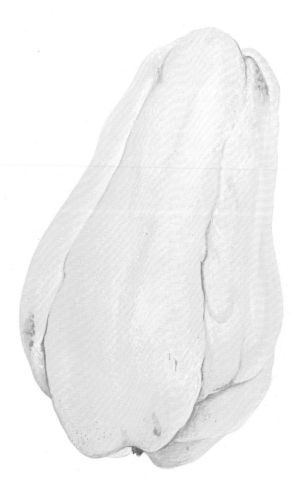

ANGLED LUFFA
Sze gwa 絲瓜

APPEARANCE: Identify this vegetable by its ridges and long thin shape. It usually measures 1–2″ in diameter, 1–2′ in length.

QUALITY: Select small, firm, young fruits, dark green in colour with tender ridges. As these gourds ripen the ridges toughen and the seeds develop undesirable properties, namely large size and purgative chemicals.

GENERAL COMMENTS: Farmers favour this variation on the summer melon theme because the plant tolerates hot humid tropical weather; cooks favour it because its texture differs slightly from that of other melons. The central flesh goes spongy, contrasting nicely with the coarse skin. Young gourds are sweet; older ones slightly bitter. (The luffa used to make sponges is a different species, known to the Cantonese as "seui gwa", 水瓜, known to the English as smooth luffa or sponge gourd.)

PREPARATION. Wash. With a vegetable scraper or small knife, remove the ridges but leave the skin between so that the result is striped. If the skin is very leathery, as happens in older gourds, remove it altogether. For stir-frying, chop the luffa diagonally and roll it as you cut in order to create wedge-shaped pieces.

COOKING:

Western. Steam, boil or sauté as you would courgettes or summer squash; season with herbs, grated Parmesan cheese, or simply butter, salt and pepper.

Chinese. Exclusively stir-fry this one. Virtually any of the combinations suggested for fuzzy melon work equally well with this. Meat (pork, beef, or chicken) and another vegetable, such as onions, spring onions, winter mushrooms, jew's ear mushrooms or fresh straw mushrooms, plus angled luffa make a common, convenient and compatible trio.

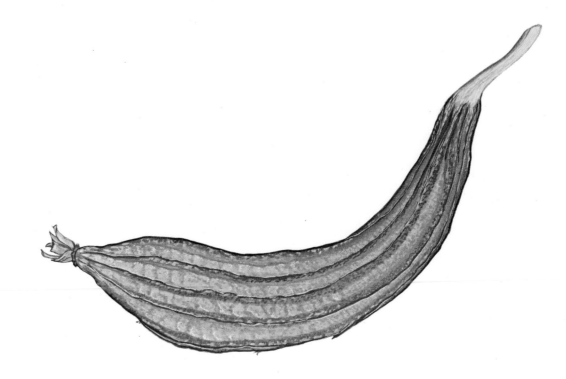

BITTER MELON
Foo gwa 苦瓜

APPEARANCE: Identify this vegetable by its warty skin. Usually 4–10″ long, its shape varies from pear-like to oblong.

QUALITY: Immature bitter melons are very green, quite bitter, but also quite firm-fleshed. Ripe melons are orange, slightly sweet and very soft. The best eating quality is somewhere in between, so select fruits which are green-turning-yellow but still firm.

GENERAL COMMENTS: Indians curry it; Ceylonese pickle it; Indonesians prefer it in cooked salads. Throughout the tropics this melon is true to its name: bitter. For some palates this is an unforgiveable sin; for others it is an endearing attribute. The keys to preparing bitter melon so that your guests fall into the latter category are: first, to pre-treat it to dispel the bitterness; and second, to season it with sweetening. The melon readily absorbs other flavours, and its bitter tang can enhance the overall taste of a dish.

PREPARATION: Asian cooks generally pre-treat bitter melon in one of two ways to reduce the bitter taste.
(1) Blanching. Wash well; halve lengthwise; remove and discard seeds. Bring water to a rolling boil, drop melon in; simmer 2–3 minutes until melon turns bright in colour; drain.
(2) Salting. Wash well, then scrape the skin lightly. Halve lengthwise; remove seeds and pith. Leave whole or slice, as recipe requires. Place melon pieces in large bowl and sprinkle with salt, about 1 teaspoon per melon. Toss lightly to coat all surfaces with salt, and let stand 15–20 minutes. Finally, rinse the melon to remove salt and bitter chemicals; squeeze dry.

COOKING:
Western. Probably the only Western vegetables comparable in taste to foo gwa are bitter greens such as dandelion or chicory leaves. All of these can be prepared similarly, one of the most popular being to sauté the vegetable (for foo gwa, after blanching) with chopped bacon, and finally to season it with salt, pepper, sugar and a dash of vinegar.
Chinese. The Cantonese prefer this vegetable stir-fried with beef or pork in black bean sauce; stuffed and fried lightly; or braised, as described below.

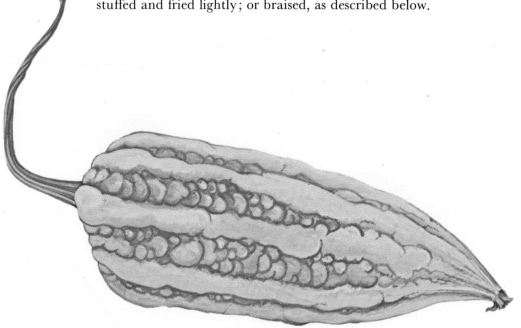

Stuffed Bitter Melon

Bitter melon, washed, halved and seeded
Pork
Dried shrimp, about 1 teaspoon per $\frac{1}{4}$ lb. of meat, soaked
Onion or spring onions
Cornstarch
(Equal parts fermented black beans and garlic, crushed and mashed together)

Mince pork, shrimps and onion together; season with salt, pepper, soy sauce, a pinch of sugar and a little oil; mix well. Blanch bitter melon; drain. When cool enough to handle chop into large squares. Dust inner surface with cornstarch to bind the filling, then spread a little filling on each.

In saucepan heat oil for sautéing. If using black beans, add the garlic-black bean mash first, then add melon squares and fry lightly. Add a little each of water, soy sauce and sugar; cover and braise until cooked. Remove to serving dish. Juices remaining in the pan may be poured over as a sauce, first thickened with cornstarch if desired.

Chicken & Melon in Fragrant Sauce

Chicken pieces
Ginger, 1 slice, crushed
Garlic, 1–2 cloves, crushed
Chinese rock sugar (bing tong 冰糖) or white or brown sugar
2 tablespoons dark soy sauce
2 tablespoons light soy sauce
(1 star anise or 1 teaspoon Chinese 5-spice powder, ng heung fun 五香粉)
1 bitter melon

In braising pot, dissolve sugar in a little water; the quantity will depend on your taste but start with about 2 tablespoons and add more later if required. Add other seasonings, and finally the chicken. Bring to a boil, cover, simmer very gently until done. Occasionally stir and baste the chicken to ensure that all pieces absorb the flavour of the sauce.

Meanwhile, wash, seed, halve and chop the melon in slices. Salt as described above, rinse, drain and squeeze dry. Add to chicken pot 15–30 minutes before serving. If sauce is too thin remove the lid towards the end of the cooking or thicken it with cornstarch.

This dish can be prepared ahead and reheated to serve. The taste improves but the bitter melon may disintegrate if cooked too long.

Furthermore, this dish can be prepared without the melon altogether. Or you can make the chicken alone one day, then use left-over chicken pieces and the sauce to braise the melon the following day.

WINTER SQUASH
Naam gwa 南瓜

APPEARANCE: Several species and innumerable varieties of winter squash exist (i.e. acorn, banana, butternut, hubbard, turban, pumpkin, etc.). Each variety differs in size, shape, skin colour, taste and texture, but all share properties of a tough outer skin, orange flesh and a central seed cavity full of edible seeds. The squash illustrated seems to be the only member of the clan grown in southern China. Its earmarks are oblong or spherical shape, 6–10″ diameter, and a faintly striped orange-tinted skin.

QUALITY: Check the stem end for rot; check the skin for worm holes, soft spots and signs of immaturity. The flesh is sweetest and most tender in fully mature (lightly frostbitten) squashes. Those picked with a bit of the stem still attached will keep the longest.

68

GENERAL COMMENTS: Winter squashes and pumpkins are native to the Americas, and only relatively recently migrated to Asia. Although becoming more popular, they will never usurp the "most-favoured" status of the white-fleshed summer melons in China. As one Cantonese expressed it: "There is a peculiar taste and [an association with pig food] that prevents it to be on higher tables."

Nevertheless, the flesh of fully mature winter squash is tender, smooth, sweet, flavourful and rich in vitamin A. Under-ripe squash are somewhat less of all of the above. Cooking times vary with the maturity of the squash and the denseness of the flesh; cooks must be careful because the stage beyond tender is mush.

A whole winter squash can keep for at least a month in the refrigerator.

PREPARATION: Cut melon in half and remove seeds and fibrous strings from the central cavity. The seeds may be separated from the fibres, washed, and dried or dry-roasted with salt to be nibbled as a snack. Leave the squash in halves for baking, or peel and chop in matchsticks for stir-frying or sautéing.

COOKING:

Western. The halves may be baked whole with a filling of butter and brown sugar or minced meat or sausage in the cavity. Pieces may be steamed, baked or boiled, then served as is, buttered, creamed, mashed or baked au gratin. Plain mashed or puréed squash can be whipped, seasoned with cream, salt and pepper; or fashioned into croquettes and deep-fried; or used as the basis of pumpkin pie.

Chinese. The Cantonese generally cook this as they do their other orange-fleshed starchy vegetables and, less commonly, as they do their summer melons. Thus, it is boiled like sweet potatoes to make a sweet soup (p. 103), or like papaya with pork or fish to make savoury soup (p. 105). Alternatively it can be stir-fried as fuzzy melon is, with chicken, or pork, or pork, onions and mushrooms, etc.

One creative Cantonese cook uses winter squash to make the following noodle dish:

Chicken Noodle Squash

In proportions to taste:
Chicken meat, chopped
Chicken liver, chopped
Winter squash, cubed
Spring onions, chopped
Shoestring rice noodles (lai fun 瀨粉)
  (Substitute: spaghetti)
Ginger and garlic, crushed

Cook noodles in boiling salted water until tender; drain; toss with a little cooked oil to prevent sticking.

In hot oil in wok, fry ginger until fragrant and remove. Add squash, stir and toss until beginning to cook, add salt and a sprinkling of water, cover and steam until tender; remove. Reheat wok with oil, fry garlic until fragrant and remove. Cook chicken; when almost done, add liver, stir and toss, return squash with spring onions as well as noodles. Cook and toss; season with light soy sauce and serve.

SWEET, GREEN OR BELL PEPPERS
Tseng jiu 青椒

APPEARANCE: Distinguish the mild bell peppers from their fiery cousins by size and shape. These measure 3–4″ in height and diameter.

QUALITY: Select firm, unblemished fruits. Check stem end for signs of rot. Those slightly red in colour are beginning to ripen and should have more vitamin C and sweetness.

GENERAL COMMENTS: The bell pepper, as a derivative of the chilli, seems to have come into cooking within the past two centuries. Nevertheless its popularity, like that of its ancestor, has spread like wildfire.

The international popularity of green peppers rests on their mild taste, bright colour and variable texture. Raw peppers are as crisp and firm as celery; stir-fried peppers are slightly more tender and succulent, while braised peppers go completely limp. Their cup-like shape and glossy, leak-proof skin particularly suit them for stuffing, which further expands the culinary possibilities of this vegetable.

PREPARATION: Wash. Remove stem with column of seeds and inner membranes. Leave whole for stuffing. For other purposes cut as desired: in rings or thin strips, Western style; or squares, Chinese style.

COOKING:

Western. Western styles of cooking bell peppers have mostly evolved in South America and in southern European countries. Peppers may be used in small quantities to season casseroles, or in larger pieces and larger proportions as a vegetable. They may be sautéd, stuffed, braised or, most simply, tossed raw in salad.

Chinese. Bell peppers are used more often in Cantonese restaurants than in Cantonese homes. Their bright colour makes them decorative; their firm texture makes them easy to store, prepare and cook; while their taste blends amenably with many other ingredients. Green and red peppers with black beans has become a standard and staple sauce for: shrimp; crab; beef and broad white rice noodles; pork ribs; squid etc. Sweet-and-sour dishes of pork or chicken and pineapple also commonly include this colourful duo.

Furthermore, versions of stuffed peppers have evolved, such as follows:

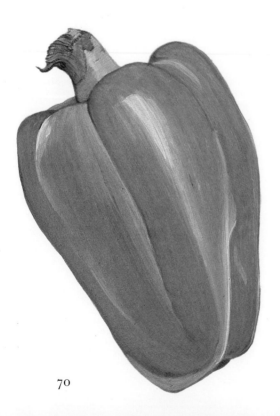

Chinese Stuffed Pepper Squares

Green peppers, cut in 1–2″ squares
Stuffing: Minced seasoned fish or lean pork; or shrimp paste as described for bean curd p. 53.
Garlic
Fermented black beans
Light and dark soy sauces

Dust pepper squares with cornstarch; spread each with stuffing.

Mash 1 part garlic together with 2 parts black beans, making about 1 tablespoon mash per 1–2 whole peppers. Heat oil in wok, fry garlic-bean paste; then lightly brown the filling side of the pepper squares. Flip; fry lightly, then add a little water, a pinch of sugar, soy sauces to taste, red chillies if desired; simmer gently 5–10 minutes. Remove pepper squares to serving dish; adjust seasoning of sauce, thicken with cornstarch and pour over the squares.

Pieces of bean curd may also be fried lightly and braised with the peppers.

Medley of Veg & Vermicelli

Mungbean vermicelli
More or less equal quantities of the following:
Preserved mustard cabbage (haam suen choi 咸酸菜, p. 23)
Lean pork, shredded and seasoned
Winter mushrooms, soaked and cut in thin strips
Green pepper, cut in thin strips
(Red chilli pepper)

Soak preserved cabbage in fresh water about 5 minutes to remove excess salt; drain; chop in shreds.

Deep-fry the dry vermicelli, a handful at a time; drain and place on serving dish. Remove all oil from wok except 2–3 tablespoons. Reheat; fry green pepper; when fragrant, add mushrooms and preserved cabbage with a dash of vinegar and a pinch of sugar; toss, then cover briefly and simmer; remove. Stir-fry meat, return vegetables; season if necessary with light soy sauce and thicken if necessary with cornstarch. Pour over vermicelli.

LEEK
Daai suen 大蒜

APPEARANCE: The shape, colour pattern and small tuft of roots at the base identify this as a member of the onion family. Its size—10–12″ long, 1″ diameter—and cylindrical, non-bulbous neck single it out as a leek.

QUALITY: Ignore the green leaves; choose individuals with as large, full, white and fresh a neck as possible.

GENERAL COMMENTS: This ancient onion is known throughout Europe and temperate Asia. It has a mild, rather sweet taste and a uniquely spongy, slippery texture.

PREPARATION: Peel off and discard outer dirty, dried or disfigured leaves and chop off upper, tough greens. This leaves the pristine white heart of the vegetable to be chopped as desired or requested by recipe.

COOKING:

Western. The French traditionally sauté leeks in butter and serve as is, in sauce, or with potatoes in soup. Alternatively, sauté then braise them briefly in sour cream with a dash of mustard; or serve them raw in any of the myriad ways spring onions are used.

Chinese. This vegetable is grown and used primarily in northern China. The Cantonese generally treat it like onions, which means, in particular, stir-fried with beef. In Peking cuisine, the heart of the leek is served as a condiment for Peking pancakes or tortillas ("bok bang," see p. 48). It is chopped in thin strips 2–3″ long and rolled with filling and sauce in pancakes to make a meal.

STEM LETTUCE
Woh sun 萵苣

APPEARANCE: At first sight identify this vegetable by its stem: 10–15″ long, 2–3″ in diameter, with prominent reddish leaf scars throughout its length. Closer inspection reveals that the leaves indeed have the oval shape, thin texture and white latex characteristic of *Lactuca*, the lettuce genus.

QUALITY: Choose individuals with the thickest stems and whitest flesh; avoid those with signs of wet rot on the leaf scars or of shrivelling.

GENERAL COMMENTS: The choicest part of this vegetable is the heart of the stem, which has a faint lettuce flavour and an unusually juicy but crisp texture.

Stem lettuce has been grown for centuries in northern China, where the leaves are cooked fresh and the stem is pickled. (N.B. This explains why Shanghai "pickled lettuce," sometimes available canned, is more like a root than a leaf in texture.) An American seed company introduced it to the West in 1942 under the name "celtuce," presumably so called because the leaves can be used like lettuce while the peeled stem is as moistly crunchy as celery.

PREPARATION: Remove leaves, wash, drain and use separately. Rinse the stem; peel off the sheath of tough outer fibres. Chop the pith as desired.

COOKING:

Western. Toss the leaves in salad. Eat the stem as is; or chop and toss in salad; or marinate with other vegetables in an Italian or oil-vinegar dressing.

Chinese. The bulk of China's stem lettuce crop goes into Shanghai pickles. You may attempt something similar by following the recipe for pickling stem ginger on p. 83, substituting light soy sauce for approximately $\frac{1}{4}$ of the vinegar.

Stem lettuce which is used fresh is generally cut in matchstick shape and stir-fried randomly with pork, poultry and/or other vegetables. Stem lettuce with peas or sugar peas, chicken and spring onions is a particularly flavourful combination.

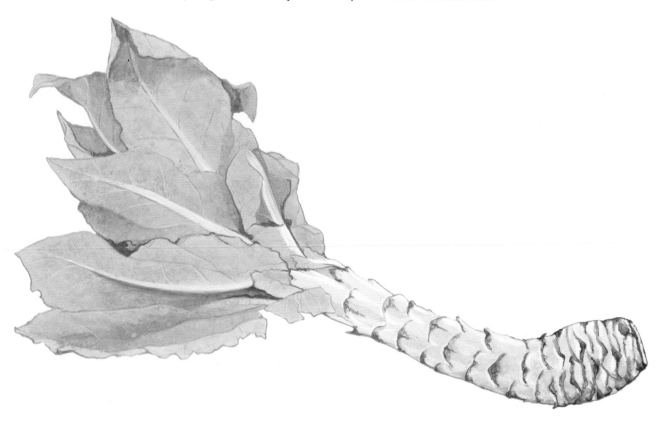

EGGPLANT
Ai gwa 矮瓜

APPEARANCE: Whatever its shape or colour, eggplant lovers everywhere will recognize this vegetable by its smooth waxy skin and the cup-shaped leaf at the stem end. In Bengal, where the plant—and apparently its name—originated, the fruits come in a variety of colours from purple to green to yellow to white, are usually ovoid and seldom more than 2″ long. Modern, cultivated varieties are typically ovoid or tubular in shape, 6–12″ long, and black, white or green in colour.

QUALITY: Buy only those which are uniformly smooth, firm and unblemished. Smaller, slightly immature individuals make the best eating.

GENERAL COMMENTS: Not unlike liver, eggplant (alias aubergine; alias brinjal) can be terrific or terrible, according to the expertise of the cook. An understanding of certain aubergenic characteristics helps ensure delectable results every time. First, eggplants benefit from a 10 minute soak in salt water before cooking, in order to remove certain subtle but objectionable bitter tastes. Second, eggplant absorbs oil—and oil-borne flavours —like a sponge. Thus you need more oil in cooking it, and slightly acid foods, such as tomatoes or vinegared sauces, complement it and that extra oil nicely. Thirdly, length of cooking time greatly affects the final texture of eggplant: cooked quickly at high temperatures, slices of eggplant absorb flavours but remain thick and succulent; cooked longer they become thin and limp.

PREPARATION: Wash well; peel if desired, either completely or in longitudinal strips for decorative effect. Slice as recipe commands, then soak in salted water or sprinkle with salt, and let rest 10–15 minutes. Rinse and squeeze before cooking.

COOKING:
Western. Indians curry it; Italians bake it with Parmesan; Greeks casserole it with cheese and lamb; while the French combine it with onions, tomatoes, green peppers and herbs in a style remarkably similar to a Chinese stir-fry. To summarize, Western cooks may sauté or bake eggplant, whole or sliced, alone or with herbs, cheese, meat or other vegetables.
Chinese. The Cantonese usually cook eggplant richly: stir-fried with black beans, braised, deep-fried in batter, or steamed and mashed with nut butter.

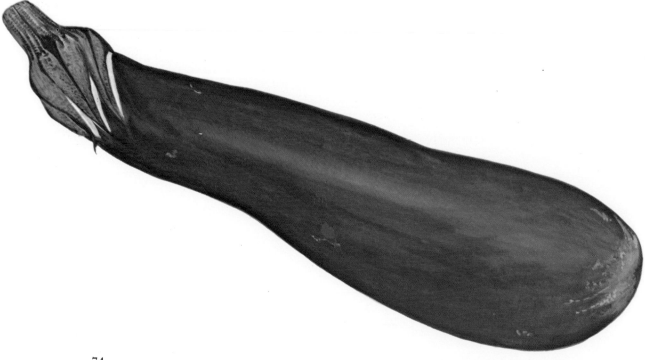

Auber-sesame

Eggplant(s)
Sauce: Sesame butter (Tsee ma jeung 芝蔴醬), tahini or peanut butter
Light soy sauce
Cooked peanut oil
(Chopped chilli peppers or chilli sauce)

Score eggplant(s) lengthwise 3–4 times; soak in salted water 10 minutes, then lay on top of rice as it steams. Meanwhile combine sauce ingredients according to taste. When eggplant is cooked soft, do one of the following:
(1) Slice it in bite-size chunks and serve with sauce for dipping or pour sauce over the chunks on serving dish;
(2) Chop and mash eggplant together with sauce until homogenous. Garnish with toasted sesame seeds or chopped peanuts and a sprig of fresh coriander to brighten an otherwise drab-looking dish.

Deep-fried Stuffed Eggplant

Stuffing: 1 cup minced fresh fish; or minced lean pork; or shrimp paste as described for bean curd, p. 53; or combination
5–6 dried shrimp, soaked and minced
2 spring onions or shallots, minced
1 teaspoon cornstarch
Combine these ingredients, with salt and white pepper to taste. To improve the final texture of the filling, form it into a ball and throw it onto the counter several times.
Batter: $\frac{1}{2}$ cup self-raising flour
or $\frac{1}{2}$ cup all-purpose flour sifted with $\frac{1}{4}$ teaspoon baking powder
1 teaspoon cornstarch
Add water to these ingredients and beat, in order to make a batter of the consistency of heavy cream.
Eggplants: Wash the eggplants then peel them in longitudinal strips, creating stripes. Slice diagonally making slices $\frac{1}{2}''$ apart and alternately slicing $\frac{3}{4}$ through (making a slit for the stuffing) and slicing all the way through.

Having prepared all of the above items, you must next stuff the eggplant. Dust both surfaces of the slit in each piece with cornstarch and spread filling in the crevice. When all have been stuffed, dip them in batter and deep-fry. Drain on paper towels. Serve immediately with saucers of vinegar for dipping.

If you have more eggplant than filling—or, alternatively, no filling at all—simply dip eggplant slices alone in batter and deep-fry; serve with vinegar dip and/or chilli sauce.

CELERY
Kunn choi 芹菜

APPEARANCE: This Chinese celery is virtually identical in form and habit to American celery but differs in size. Whole stalks of Chinese celery are less compact, and individual stalks seldom measure more than $\frac{1}{2}''$ in diameter or more than 10″ in length.

QUALITY: Select plants with the fattest and whitest (i.e., most tender) stalks. Check for worm holes in cracks in the stalks.

GENERAL COMMENTS: Apparently both Euro-American and Chinese celeries are the same species and represent divergent development over 1,500 years. Both have the same aromatic flavour and crisp, externally stringy texture; the Chinese type is simply stronger in both respects. Use the latter more sparingly and chop it more finely otherwise it successfully resists chewing.

The Cantonese traditionally include their celery in vegetarian dishes served during the Chinese Lunar New Year. To eat "kunn choi" on the first day of the year should give a person "kunn lik," (勤力, i.e. diligence to work hard); and furthermore, if it is eaten with the black hair seaweed "faat choi" (髮菜), this diligence will undoubtedly bring ever-increasing (i.e. "faat" 發) wealth (i.e. "choi" 財).

PREPARATION: Separate leaf stalks and wash well. Remove the string-like fibres in the tops of the ridges running lengthwise on each stalk. Chop as desired, preferably in matchsticks or long diagonals for Chinese stir-frying.

COOKING:

Western. Westerners eat celery both raw and cooked, as seasoning and as vegetable. This variety is best suited for the latter purposes because of its tough fibres (unless, of course, your guests have knife-edged teeth). A leaf or two enhances the flavour of soups and broths; the cooked stalks can be served as a side-dish or puréed as the base of a cream soup.

Chinese. The Cantonese cook "faan kunn choi," foreign or American celery, far more often than their native celery, presumably because of the former's milder taste and more tender texture, Nevertheless, either can be stir-fried with other meats, poultry, vegetables (particularly mungbean sprouts) or seafood (particularly squid).

New Year's Prosperity Dish

1 cup Chinese celery, chopped in 1″ lengths
¼ cup dried black hair seaweed (faat choi 髮菜)
10 deep-fried wheat puffs (sang gunn 生筋)
1 slice fresh ginger, crushed
1 tablespoon oyster sauce

Soak seaweed in water to cover for 30 minutes or more; rinse and drain. Parboil wheat puffs to remove dirt and excess oil; drain.

To cook, heat oil in wok and season with ginger; when oil is very hot add celery. Stir and toss until fragrant and beginning to look cooked, then add seaweed and wheat puffs. Season with oyster sauce, add ½ cup water or light stock, cover and simmer strongly 3–4 minutes. Adjust seasoning. Sauce should by now be thick; if not, quickly boil down or thicken with cornstarch; serve.

Celery & Squid

Equal quantities of squid and celery, chopped in long but thin diagonals
1 slice fresh ginger, crushed
Wine or cooking sherry
(Sesame oil)

To prepare squid: Remove head with tendrils; discard head but save tendrils. Strip purplish skin from body and remove its single white, plate-like bone. Lay remaining rectangular section of squid on cutting board, skin side up. With sharp knife score it in a grid pattern, and finally cut in rectangles approximately 1 × ½″ in size.

To cook the dish: In hot oil in wok, stir-fry celery and remove. Add more oil, fry ginger until fragrant and discard. Add squid; toss until pieces curl and turn white. Sprinkle with wine or sherry, season with salt, white pepper and a dash of sugar. Return celery with any juices which might have accumulated from it. Toss and simmer furiously to blend flavours. Add a drop or two of sesame oil if convenient, thicken sauce with cornstarch if desired, and serve.

BAMBOO SHOOTS
Chuk sun 竹筍

APPEARANCE: There are as many different kinds of bamboo shoots as there are kinds of bamboo—and at least ten of the possible hundred or so are marketed. The shoots fall into two broad categories: spring shoots, as illustrated here, which measure an impressive 3–5″ in diameter at the base and 10″ or more in length; and winter shoots, which are only half as large but otherwise look identical.

QUALITY: Each species of bamboo shoot has its own characteristic flavour and degree of sweetness, as well as size and season. Generally, winter types are considered more choice than spring; within any type, smaller shoots should be more tender and yellower (less green) ones sweeter.

GENERAL COMMENTS: The uses of bamboo among Oriental people are ancient and legion. Baskets, hats, houses, chopsticks, paper, pipes, pots and, of course, food are among its products. For centuries poets and painters have tried to capture its beauty, while gardeners and farmers have been trying to nip its buds. Fresh bamboo shoots are mildly sweet in taste, crunchy in texture, and far superior in both respects to their canned counterparts. Originally this was a northern vegetable, popular in the cuisines of Peking and Shanghai. The shoots appear commonly in northern, wheat-based foods (noodle dishes, wonton, dumpling stuffings, etc.) and in vegetarian dishes, but rarely on average Cantonese dinner tables. Restaurants of all sorts tend to use bamboo shoots ubiquitously for their pleasant texture, mild taste and amenability to fancy carving.

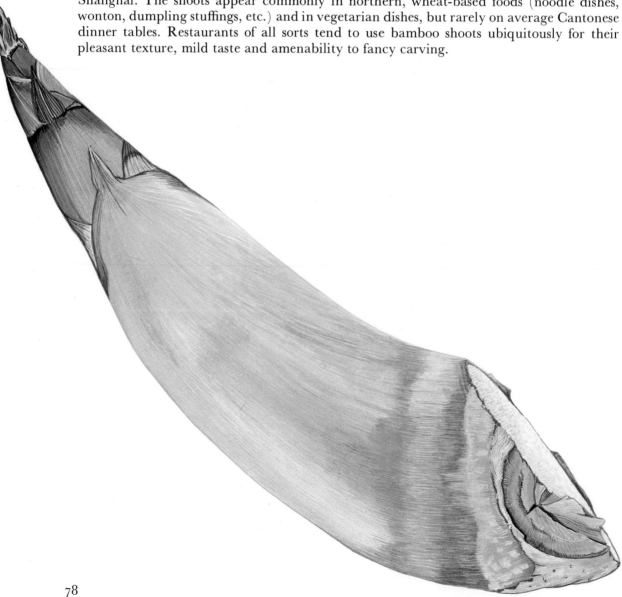

78

PREPARATION: Fresh bamboo shoots contain a bitter poison, hydrocyanic acid, which must be destroyed before they are eaten. Parboiling is the accepted method of handling this problem. To prepare bamboo shoots for cooking, first strip off all leaves. Then, using a sharp, thin knife, slice off and discard the tough base. The central core is the edible bit, so slice it into appropriately bite-sized rectangles. Bring a large pot of water to a rolling boil; add sliced shoots, boil 5 minutes, drain, rinse and sample. If shoots still taste bitter, repeat the boiling process; otherwise proceed.

Refrigerated, unpeeled bamboo shoots will keep at least a week. You can peel, slice and parboil the end gradually as needed, or you can prepare the whole shoot at once and refrigerate or freeze unused pieces for use later.

Canned bamboo shoots may be used straight from the can after rinsing.

COOKING:

Western. After parboiling, bamboo shoots may be served immediately as a side dish; sautéd, baked or creamed with other vegetables; marinated; or chilled and tossed in lettuce salads. *Chinese.* Bamboo shoots can probably be used to advantage in any vegetable or vegetable and meat combination stir-fry. They are particularly useful for contrast—in texture, when cooked with softer vegetables such as the melons, Peking cabbage, fresh mushrooms, etc.; or in colour, when cooked with brightly coloured vegetables such as green beans.

One of the most esteemed dishes using bamboo shoots is the following:

Seung Dong Choi 雙冬菜

Bamboo shoots, chopped and parboiled
Winter mushrooms
(Lean pork, shredded and seasoned)

Use approximately equal parts bamboo shoots and mushrooms, using pork in quantity as desired for flavour. Most authentically, both mushrooms and bamboo shoots are deep-fried separately first, then combined and braised briefly in stock, seasoned with sugar, soy sauce and a little wine.

Alternatively, you may stir-fry them, add the mushroom-soaking liquid and simmer until cooked and thoroughly flavoured, 15–30 minutes. Remove; fry the pork, return the vegetables, heat through, adjust seasoning with soy sauce, and serve.

STRAW MUSHROOMS
Tso gwoo 草菇

APPEARANCE: Smooth, grey and brown nubs about 1″ long can be none other than straw (or grass) mushrooms. Very fresh, they are light in colour, soundly and roundly firm. With age they darken, become slightly slimy on the outside, and pop their tops as the umbrella-like mushrooms grow through the membranes which enclose them.

QUALITY: Choose the youngest, i.e. those which are pale in colour, small in size, and hard or uniformly firm in texture, with no sign of an erupting umbrella.

GENERAL COMMENTS: The name of this mushroom derives from the fact that it was originally cultivated on rice-straw; modern farmers have discovered it does equally well on fertilized cotton wool but the old name sticks. "Tso gwoo" are comparable to the field or button mushrooms of the West in taste, texture and ease of mass production. The most conspicuous difference between the two is growth form, as button mushrooms grow like an umbrella while straw mushrooms grow like an umbrella inside a case. Either way, the taste is mild and the texture smooth and firm, not unlike succulent rubber.

    These mushrooms are difficult to store. Whether in the fridge or out, in a plastic bag or ventilated basket, they soon begin to deteriorate. Plan to use them within two days of purchase.

PREPARATION: Wash well, especially the lower ends. Trim as needed; peeling is unnecessary.

COOKING:

Western. Straw mushrooms can substitute for Western button mushrooms in virtually any recipe except those requiring a cap—for instance, for stuffing. Slice them, or leave whole; sauté in butter, possibly with herbs or spices; combine with meats and other vegetables in casseroles; or use as the foundation for cream of mushroom soup.

Chinese. These are the only mushrooms which the Cantonese commonly eat fresh. Generally, they serve them whole, either braised or boiled. (Beware that this is easier said than done because using chopsticks to retrieve sauce-coated tso gwoo from a platter requires considerable manual dexterity.) Again generally, straw mushrooms are cooked with other delicately flavoured ingredients, such as fish, shellfish, bean curd and lettuce, although they go equally well with the rich flavour of a black bean sauce.

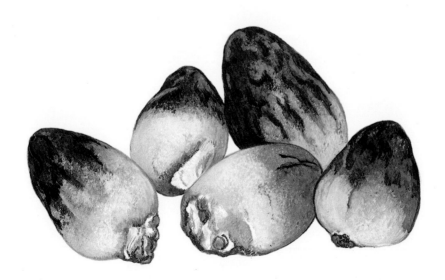

Mushrooms & Ribs in Black Bean Sauce

1 lb. pork ribs, chopped in 1–2″ lengths, seasoned
½ lb. straw mushrooms
3–4 cloves garlic, crushed
1–2 tablespoons fermented black beans

Mash garlic and beans together. In hot oil in wok, fry this paste until fragrant; add pork ribs. Toss until browned; add a pinch of sugar, dashes of light and dark soy sauce, and water to cover to about ⅓; simmer until cooked. Add mushrooms; simmer another 3–4 minutes until mushrooms are cooked as well. Adjust seasoning; if sauce seems too thin thicken it with cornstarch; serve.

Braised Mushrooms and Crab

2 cups straw mushrooms
1 cup crab meat, flaked into shreds
1½ cups light stock, or water and a chicken stock cube
Seasoning: Cooking wine; sesame oil; white pepper; cornstarch
(Lettuce, one of the Chinese cabbages, or other green vegetable)

(Stir-fry green vegetable and arrange on a serving dish.)

In wok or saucepan, simmer mushrooms in stock. When cooked add crab meat with dashes of wine, sesame oil and white pepper to taste; continue to simmer until flavours are thoroughly blended. Thicken sauce with 1 tablespoon cornstarch mixed to a paste with a little water. Adjust seasoning with salt. Serve as is, or pour over green vegetable as a sauce; you may further garnish the dish with fresh coriander, chopped spring onions or green peas.

STEM GINGER
Tsee geung 子薑

APPEARANCE: The knobby shape and moist, pink, rather naked appearance of this vegetable distinguish it immediately. The shape is characteristically irregular, but generally oblong and jointed; each knob is about $\frac{1}{2}''$ in diameter with bright pink collars of leaf sheaths at the base of new shoots.

QUALITY: The older the more fibrous; thus select pieces with many pink young buds and smooth, clear, yellow flesh.

GENERAL COMMENTS: Stem ginger is the newest spring growth of the ginger rhizome (a rhizome being an underground stem). Old, mellowed ginger with its dry, brown skin is used as a seasoning, but these young upstarts are eaten as a vegetable or as a pickle. They have a fresh, fragrant, gingery flavour with a tenderly crisp texture.

PREPARATION: Scrape surface lightly using a small knife with its blade held perpendicular to the ginger's surface; rinse. For pickling, chop at the joints into chunks of convenient size. For stir-frying, slice as thinly as possible across the grain with long diagonal cuts. In either case, place the bits in a large bowl, sprinkle with salt and toss to mix. Cantonese cooks maintain that the ginger will have a crisper texture, with less bruises, if tossed rather than mixed with a spoon or a hand. To toss, grasp the side of the bowl with both hands and flick your wrists quickly but gently.

COOKING:

Western. For variety of texture and less pungent flavour, add minced stem ginger to ginger snaps and gingerbread and, with raisins and candied fruit peel, to fruitcakes, spice cookies, bread puddings, etc. Pickled ginger makes an interesting addition to salads, particularly with yoghurt, cucumber and water chestnuts.

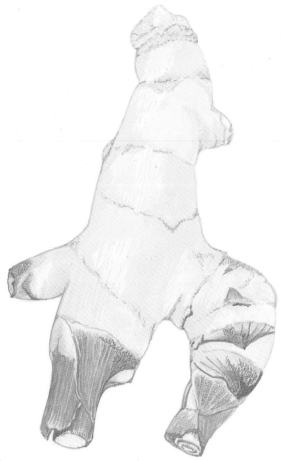

82

Chinese. Probably the largest part of Canton's stem ginger crop is preserved in sugar and exported to Western countries in "ginger jars" as a sweetmeat. Most Cantonese, however, withdraw in polite distaste from the very idea of sweet ginger and prefer instead to eat theirs pickled. Thin slices of pickled ginger with preserved duck egg (pei daan 皮蛋) is a common snack, an hors d'oeuvre served by some restaurants, and a quick dinner dish to accompany rice. Stem ginger—either before or after pickling—may be stir-fried, with chicken, with chicken and melon, or, most traditionally, with beef.

Pickled Ginger

1 lb. stem ginger
1 tablespoon salt
2 cups white vinegar
1 clove garlic, crushed
$2\frac{1}{4}$ cups white granulated sugar

Wash, scrape, rinse and salt ginger as described above. Toss it 5–6 times every 5 minutes for 20 minutes. The salt will draw juice from the ginger so that the finished pickles will be crisp. Meanwhile bring the vinegar to the boil; add a pinch of salt, the garlic and the sugar. Simmer gently 3–4 minutes until the sugar is dissolved and the garlic has disseminated its flavour. Sample the brew and adjust its sweet-to-sour balance to your own taste.

When the ginger is ready, blot each piece dry with paper towels. Place in a clean bowl or hot jars and pour hot pickling liquid over; all ginger should be immersed. When cool, pack in jars and refrigerate.

The pickles should turn pink and be crisp. To ensure success chill finished ginger within three hours, and use jars with non-metal lids as the vinegar will quickly corrode metal.

The ginger will be ready to eat within 3–5 days, depending on the size of the knobs of ginger, and will keep at least a year in the fridge.

Beef & Stem Ginger

1–2″ of stem ginger or comparable quantity pickled ginger
Approximately twice this volume of beef, sliced thinly across the grain and seasoned
(Chinese chives flower stalks or spring onions, chopped in 1″ lengths)

If using fresh stem ginger, prepare it for stir-frying as described above. After tossing with salt, let it rest 5–10 minutes, then rinse well and blot dry. Heat oil in wok, add ginger, stir and toss 2 minutes, add onions, stir and cook until shiny and fragrant; remove. Reheat oil in wok, sear beef quickly, return vegetables with a little water if necessary. Stir and toss to blend flavours; adjust seasoning with light soy sauce, and dish.

If using pickled ginger, sear beef, then add ginger with a little pickling juice or water, simmer to blend flavours, thicken with cornstarch if necessary, and dish.

WILD RICE SHOOTS
Gaau sun 膠荀

APPEARANCE: The spear shape with overlapping, wrapping leaves marks this vegetable as a young shoot; its 10–15″ length, 1–2″ diameter and light colouring unmistakably earmark it as a shoot of wild rice. The example illustrated here has been cut in half to show the pattern of black dots seen in cross-section which also characterizes this vegetable.

QUALITY: Select firm, fresh shoots with bases of large diameter. Since only the solid pith of the stem is eaten, the larger the stem the greater the proportion of food per stalk.

GENERAL COMMENTS: The texture of wild rice shoots is comparable to a cross between potatoes and eggplant: firm yet sponge-like and moist. It has little inherent flavour but readily absorbs and enhances the flavours of foods with which it associates. A botanist travelling (and eating) in China in 1913 asserted that: "From a European standpoint [gaau sun] is really very good eating."

   The wild rice plant producing these shoots, in fact, seems to be the same species which the Indians of North America have traditionally cultivated for grain and which is now known as "wild rice." The plant occurs through the middle of Asia, from Japan to Indo-China, but is consistently cultivated there as a vegetable rather than as a grain crop. It is of a different genus altogether from true or ordinary rice.

PREPARATION: Peel off and discard all leaves. Slice inner shoot in long diagonals for stir-frying, or otherwise as desired.

COOKING:
Western. Sauté; bake; steam and serve buttered, sauced, or tossed with bits of bacon or ham.
Chinese. As with other less common vegetables the Cantonese serve this one simply: usually stir-fried with shreds of lean pork, preceded by bits of garlic and ginger to season the oil. In this way the taste of the shoots perform solo; for orchestration, add thin slices of other vegetables such as onion or green pepper.

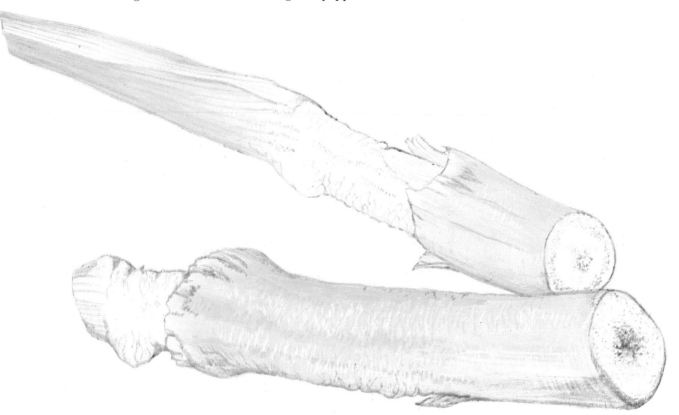

DRACONTOMELUM
Yun meen 人面

APPEARANCE: These small fruits measure about $\frac{1}{2}''$ in diameter; they are almost as solid as nuts, with thick leathery skin.

QUALITY: Choose the smallest ones, without signs of rot, shrivelling or worms.

GENERAL COMMENTS: Dracontomelum is the fruit of a wild tropical tree of the same botanical family as mango, cashew and pistachio. Roughly 50% of each fruit is resinous, sour skin; 10% is sour white pulp; and the rest is immature seed. The white seed has a lozenge-shape and prominent grooves and dents in various patterns. On some seeds these markings resemble those of a human face, hence the Cantonese name, "yun," meaning person, and "meen," meaning face. An English equivalent might be "man-in-the-moon fruit."

PREPARATION: Wash.

COOKING:
Among Cantonese the dish described below is universally recommended as the best way to serve dracontomelums.

Minced Pork & Dracontomelum

Pork meat, minced, chopped or shredded, and seasoned
Stem ginger
Dracontomelums*
Salted yellow bean paste (meen see 麵豉)
Sugar

As for quantities, the relative proportions of these ingredients vary greatly from cook to cook. Some use approximately equal quantities, with a little more pork, a little less dracontomelum, and just a bit of sugar. Others use 4 parts ginger: 3 parts pork: 2 parts dracontomelum: 1 part meen see: $\frac{1}{2}$ part sugar. "Chacun à son goût," but methods are the same.

Crush yun meen fruits with sharp, heavy blows of the flat side of a cleaver; mince. Similarly crush, mince or finely shred the ginger. Thoroughly mix all ingredients. Place in shallow dish and steam until pork is cooked, about 15 minutes. Dribble a little cooked oil over, and serve.

*You may substitute green pickled olives. The taste is different, of course, but the effect is sufficiently similar to be worth mentioning.

LOTUS ROOT
Leen ngau 蓮藕

APPEARANCE: This vegetable looks like strings of fat sausages. The swollen bulbs are 2–3″ in diameter and 6–10″ long, separated by narrow "necks." They are quite hard, usually dirty (evidence of their muddy-pond habitat) and decoratively hollow.

QUALITY: Examine carefully, despite the mud, to select whole, unblemished roots. If the surface is punctured dirt gets inside and makes the roots very difficult to clean.

GENERAL COMMENTS: The lotus is another ancient, symbol-ridden, and multi-purpose Oriental food. The flowers, rising from filthy roots to blossom in pristine splendour, are revered as a hopeful symbol of man's eventual rebirth. While waiting for this event, seedpods are used as medicine; seeds are puréed to make sweets and boiled whole in tonic soups; and the leaves become fragrant wrappers for steamed foods. The root is served as a vegetable. Its flavour is mildly sweet, its texture crunchy, and its appearance exotic. In cross-section, the canals of the bulb (properly termed "rhizome," a sort of subterranean stem) create a lacy pattern which can embellish any dish.

   Canned lotus root substitutes reasonably well for fresh. It is not quite as crisp or tasty but requires less time to cook.

PREPARATION: Wash and scrub well. Chop off and discard the necks between bulbs. Peel away the thin outer skin. Chop as desired: slices are decorative but chunks fit the mouth better and seem to be more typically Cantonese.

86

COOKING:

Western. Like other starchy vegetables, lotus root may be boiled, baked, braised or, in thin slices, sautéd for deep-fried.

Chinese. For special occasions whole lotus roots are stuffed with seasoned mashed mung-beans and braised with pork. During the Lunar New Year season, slices of lotus root and other vegetables such as carrot and winter melon are candied and served as snacks. Most commonly, however, the roots are boiled in soup or braised with pork. Fatter cuts of meat are usually used to complement the starchiness of the vegetable.

For unusual flavour, as seems appropriate for this exotic vegetable, try the following:

Braised Pork and Lotus

Pork: either meat, spare ribs or pig's trotter
Lotus root, peeled, chopped or sliced
*Fermented red bean curd (Naam yue 南乳), $\frac{1}{4}$–$\frac{1}{2}$ square per large bulb of lotus
(Peanuts)

In braising pot, brown pork and lotus in oil. Add bean curd (peanuts) and water to about $\frac{1}{2}''$ deep. Cover and simmer on low heat until lotus and meat are tender. Stir occasionally and add water as necessary to prevent sticking or burning. Adjust seasoning with soy sauce and serve.

Because the "naam yue" tends to preserve the other ingredients, this dish will keep for at least a week in the fridge, and will improve in flavour as it keeps.

*A combination of equal parts dark and light soy sauce may be substituted for the "naam yue", but the taste will be completely different, the sauce will have to be thickened with corn-starch, and you should omit the peanuts.

Octo-pork Soup

1 small dried octopus (cheung yue 章魚)
$\frac{1}{2}$ lb. pork bones
6–10" of lotus root, well scrubbed

As illustrated, the octopus will measure 5–6" long and will be held stretched open by a small stick of wood. Remove the wood; rinse the octopus. Remove the necks between lotus bulbs, but otherwise leave the lotus whole. Combine all ingredients in a large pot with at least twice as much water. Boil at least 2 hours. Season with salt and serve.

TARO
Woo tau 芋頭

APPEARANCE: Hairy brown skin with encircling rings and uniform oval shape distinguish taro from other vegetables. Within that category there are many varieties, of which two are illustrated here:
Betel-nut Taro (Bun long woo tau 檳榔芋頭): large, measuring up to 4″ in diameter; and
Red-budded Taro (Hung nga woo tau 紅芽芋頭): small, measuring 1–2″ in diameter, about the same size and shape as a large duck egg.

QUALITY: Look between the hairs to be sure tubers are full and wormless. Buds, if present, should be small and bright pink in colour.

GENERAL COMMENTS: In the 2,000 years that Asians, Africans and Polynesians have been cultivating taro, more than 200 varieties have been developed. All appear to belong to one species, in two main subgroups: the dasheen of Trinidad and the West Indies which produces a large central tuber (like the betel-nut taro); and the eddoe, which produces many smaller tubers (like the red-budded taro).

In general, like potato, taro is a starchy tuber of bland taste. The many varieties differ in appearance as well as flavour and texture, but certain broad characteristics remain constant. The skin is hairy and brown; the flesh may vary in colour from white to purplish; all parts contain calcium oxalate which must be cooked to be eaten safely; its texture is smooth and creamy due to exceedingly small starch grains, which are also easy to digest. Nutritionally, taro has slightly more protein and minerals than its counterpart the potato.

PREPARATION: The small taros may be left whole for baking or boiling. The larger ones must be peeled and chopped. Some people with sensitive skin are allergic to the oxalate crystals in raw taro; if this is your case, wear rubber gloves.

COOKING:

Western. Taro substitutes admirably for potatoes in almost any recipe. It may be boiled, buttered, mashed, baked, sautéd, creamed, deep-fried or stewed. The smaller variety is particularly tender and choice. It is comparable, even in appearance, to new potatoes and is, comparably, perhaps best appreciated when served simply boiled and buttered. The larger taro is slightly drier and coarser in texture, so benefits from long cooking or braising with slightly fatty cuts of meat.

Chinese. The traditional Cantonese way of eating small red-budded taros is to boil them in their jackets, peel and eat them out of hand by the light of the full moon at the Mid-Autumn Festival. At other times the two varieties are interchangeable in recipes for braising, steaming or frying, as described below.

Sweet Braised Taro

2–3 cups taro, peeled and chopped in chunks
1 large clove of garlic, crushed
1–2 tablespoons black beans
$\frac{1}{2}$–1 cup pork (preferably half fat-half lean), chopped
2–3 teaspoons dark soy sauce
1–2 teaspoons light soy sauce

Mash garlic with black beans. Heat oil in wok; fry bean mash; add pork to sear briefly, then add taro. Stir and cook until lightly browned. Transfer to saucepan; add soy sauces with 1 teaspoon (or more) sugar and $\frac{1}{2}$–1 cup water. Simmer 30–45 minutes or until taro is tender. Stir occasionally and add water as necessary to prevent burning. Adjust seasoning and serve.

Steamed Pork & Taro

$1\frac{1}{2}$ cups taro, peeled, coarsely grated
$\frac{1}{2}$ cup lean pork, minced, seasoned
Additional ingredients as desired:
    Winter mushrooms, soaked, chopped
    Bamboo shoots, chopped
    Dried shrimp, soaked, minced

Combine all ingredients. Add approximately $\frac{1}{4}$ cup hot water, season with salt, pepper, a piece of a chicken stock cube, 1 tablespoon cooked oil and $\frac{1}{2}$–1 teaspoon cornstarch. Mix well. Place in shallow dish or enamel pan; steam over boiling water or cooking rice until pork is cooked.

Savoury Taro Pudding ("Woo Tau Go" 芋頭糕)

Follow the directions and recipe for Loh Baak Go, p. 91, except substitute small cubes of taro for the grated radish and omit the sesame seed and ginger garnish.

This pudding is less common than the radish version, but is smoother in texture and more flavourful.

ORIENTAL RADISH
Loh baak 蘿蔔

APPEARANCE: The hallmarks of this root are its large size (seldom less than 5″ in length), smooth skin and generally alabaster colour. It is usually cylindrical like a carrot, although some Japanese varieties resemble soccer balls in size and shape.

QUALITY: Heavy, solid, unblemished individuals are best. Inside they should be solid, not fibrous, somewhat translucent and pungently smelling of radish.

GENERAL COMMENTS: The Japanese call this vegetable "daikon;" botanists describe it as a centuries-old cultivated variety of the small round red salad radish. Your nose and taste buds will assure you that those who call it "Chinese turnip" are wrong. The flesh is crisp, juicy, mildly pungent in taste, and edible raw or cooked.

PREPARATION: Wash and scrape the surface lightly to peel; chop as desired.

COOKING:

Western. Westerners may enjoy this vegetable best sliced thinly in salads. It can also be pickled in vinegar with sugar and a little chilli pepper. To pickle "loh baak," follow the recipe for pickling stem ginger (p. 83) except slice the radish in thin cross-sections or shreds before salting.

Chinese. "Loh Baak Go" 蘿蔔糕 is one of the most common concoctions made from this vegetable. A "go" 糕 is a stiff rice flour pudding which is mixed, steamed, cooled, then sliced in squares and fried lightly just before serving. There are both sweet and savoury types; "loh baak go" is savoury, made of grated radish, and minced seasonings such as roast pork or sausage, winter mushrooms and dried shrimps. Cantonese restaurants serve it as a dim sum, while housewives prepare it to serve to guests and family at Chinese New Year.

Besides this, loh baak may be stir-fried, braised or boiled. To stir-fry, first toss the prepared slices with salt and let drain 10–20 minutes to keep them crisp; then cook with rich cuts of meat, under a highly flavoured meat sauce or in a traditional combination with pickled pig's feet and black beans.

For braising and boiling, use loh baak as you would potatoes: with carrots and beef to make a hearty winter soup, or braised, like stew, with cuts which require long cooking such as shin of beef or pork skin. The radish withstands long cooking without disintegrating, absorbs the meat flavours, improves the sauce and possibly helps tenderize the meat as well.

Hearty Winter Soup
1 Oriental radish, peeled and chopped in chunks
Carrots, equal weight, similarly peeled and chopped
Soup meat or soup bones, beef or pork
1 handful dried figs, if using pork and if desired

Combine all ingredients in large pot; add a slice of fresh ginger if handy and 2–3 times as much water as volume of ingredients. Boil several hours until broth is well flavoured. Season with salt and pepper.

Braised Beef & Radish

Oriental radish, peeled and chopped in chunks
Stewing beef, chopped in similarly sized chunks
5-spice powder (ng heung fun 五香粉) or 1–2 star anise

In small amount of oil in braising pot, brown meat. Add radish, spice powder (1–2 teaspoons per pound of meat, or according to taste and pungency of powder), and water to a depth of 1″. Cover and simmer gently until meat is tender. Adjust seasoning with salt or soy sauce and serve.

Alternatively, but perhaps with less flavour, the meat can be braised alone and poured over parboiled loh baak to serve.

Radish Pudding ("Loh Baak Go" 蘿蔔糕)

Ingredients:[1]
5–6 lbs. radish
1 lb. rice flour (tsim mei fun 粘米粉)
4 sticks of Chinese sausage (laap cheung 臘腸) or about 1 cup Cantonese roast pork (char siu 叉燒), fresh pork meat, or possibly ham
½ cup dried shrimp, soaked
5–10 winter mushrooms, soaked
1 strip Chinese barbecued fat pork (laap yuk 臘肉) or 1 cup fat pork
2 dried halibut (tsoh hau yue 左口魚) or 1 chicken stock cube
¼ cup preserved red ginger (hung geung 紅薑), finely shredded
¼–½ cup toasted sesame seeds

Method: To make soup stock, toast fish directly over a flame or under a grill, ignoring minor burns, and then simmer it in about 4 cups of water about 30 minutes.

Meanwhile, grate radish coarsely and directly into water (but not too much) otherwise it will discolour. Add water to barely cover it, and simmer about 15 minutes. Chop meats in small dice, chop mushrooms in even smaller dice, and mince shrimps.

Drain fish and radish; combine liquids in a large pot where they will cool slightly. Put rice flour in a large bowl; add soaking liquid from mushrooms and cooked stock gradually, stirring constantly; add water as necessary to make a batter of medium viscosity. Season to taste with about a tablespoon of salt and some white pepper.

Combine batter, cooked radish (discard the fish), mushrooms, shrimp, sausage and pork in large wok or pot. Heat, *stirring constantly*, until mixture begins to thicken. Pour into two oiled 10″ diameter × 2″ deep pans, or any number of smaller pans (such as cake pans) of the necessary volume; steam 1½–2 hours until thoroughly set. Add more water as needed.[2] When done, sprinkle thickly with sesame seeds, scatter shreds of ginger over and steam an additional 5–10 minutes.

Serve the pudding immediately or, as is more common among Cantonese, let it cool. Later slice it in ½″ thick slabs, fry lightly (giving the outside a thin, crisp crust while softening the inside) and serve for breakfast, lunch or dinner. "Go" should be solid enough to slice, but not dry or pasty; added ingredients should be evenly distributed throughout and should subtly but richly flavour the otherwise mild radish.

---

[1] You may, of course, halve or quarter the recipe. You may alter the proportions and amounts of ingredients to taste; you may alter the ingredients altogether if you like the idea.

[2] This step is highly variable. For steaming, if your wok or pot is deep enough, set the bottom pan on a rack or brick and stack the other(s) on top of it by using two wooden chopsticks laid parallel across the rim of the bottom pan as a rack. Only the depth of your pot and supply of chopsticks limit stacking in this manner.

Lacking a large pot, you may steam it like English sweet puddings in the oven, or bake it in loaf pans. In the latter case, use a low temperature such as 300° F, cover the pans with foil, and set a pan of water in the oven to create a moist environment.

GREEN ORIENTAL RADISH
Tseng loh baak 青蘿蔔

APPEARANCE: Like many of the white Oriental radishes, this vegetable is tubular in shape, 6–8″ or more in length, usually about 2″ in diameter—but green in colour, both inside and out.

QUALITY: Sound, heavy roots are the best; avoid those scarred by worm holes or with signs of rot at the stem end.

GENERAL COMMENTS: This is another cultivated variety of the radish, with the same crisp texture and mildly pungent taste but in a different colour. The Cantonese use this for soup, with either beef, pork or fish, and always with carrot.

COOKING:

This radish may be substituted for the others with only visual differences. The following is a tonic soup prepared by Cantonese mothers to help their families combat the effects of dry weather (e.g. less than 70% relative humidity):

Dry Weather Soup

2 fish
$\frac{1}{2}$ lb. pork meat or 1 lb. pork bones
3 dried Chinese jujubes (mut joe 蜜棗)
1 green radish, peeled, coarsely chopped
Carrot, equal quantity to the radish, also coarsely chopped

Scale, gut, wash, drain, pat dry and rub the fish lightly with salt. Sauté in oil (preferably with a slice of fresh ginger) until golden. Combine all ingredients in large pot with 2–3 times as much water; bring to a boil and simmer until broth is milky white and well flavoured. Season with salt and white pepper; serve.

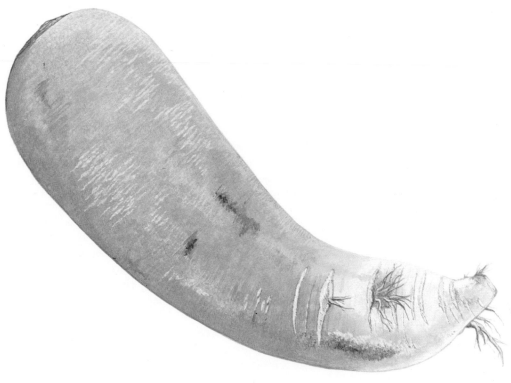

ARROWHEAD TUBERS
Tsee goo 慈菇

APPEARANCE: These tubers resemble small eggs in size, shape and colour. They measure about $1\frac{1}{2}''$ in length and $1''$ in diameter. Smooth, beige skin with peeling brown leaves distinguish them from other root vegetables of similar dimensions.

QUALITY: Select firm, fully rounded, sound tubers with as small a sprout as possible.

GENERAL COMMENTS: Like other starchy tubers, arrowheads have a bland taste, sweetened by high carbohydrate content. Farmers of Szechuan and Yunnan provinces of China grow more of them than anyone else.

PREPARATION: Peel off outer skin down to white flesh; remove sprout. Leave whole for braising or slice as desired.

COOKING:

Western. Use arrowhead tubers as you would potatoes, but expect a smoother texture and slightly different taste. They may be served whole like new potatoes; chopped and fried like hashbrowns; mashed; creamed; or baked. Add herbs and/or spring onions for flavour and colour.

Chinese. During cold weather, braised arrowhead tubers are a popular dish among Cantonese. The recipe is basically the same as that for Braised Taro, p. 89; for variety you may substitute salted yellow bean paste (meen see 麵豉) for the black beans, or leave either out altogether, flavouring only with soy sauces.

KOHLRABI
Gaai laan tau 芥蘭頭

APPEARANCE: Botanically this vegetable is a swollen stem. It is as hard as a root, 2–4″ in diameter, light green to purplish-red in colour, with or without leaves attached to the stalks which protrude from the stem.

QUALITY: Choose solid, unblemished plants; the smaller the more tender because old plants tend to become woody. Green or red, colour seems unrelated to eating quality.

GENERAL COMMENTS: The flesh of kohlrabi is white, firm and crisp with a pungency in taste characteristic of the cabbages. It may be eaten raw or cooked.

Kohlrabi, cauliflower and common head cabbage are all varieties of a single species, and all are relatively recent introductions to Asia. Nevertheless, kohlrabi is gaining popularity because it is easy to grow, and therefore inexpensive, and because it tastes much like the choice pith of its namesake, "gaai laan" (Chinese kale).

PREPARATION: First, remove any leaves left on the plant and reserve for cooking separately. To eat raw, wash stem and peel away the fibrous outer skin, including leaf bases. Slice inner heart as desired.

To braise or boil, peel and chop in chunks.

For other cooking, parboil the vegetable first—preferably whole and unpeeled to retain maximum flavour and nutrition. Bring salted water to the boil, add the washed kohlrabi and continue to boil until not quite tender or thoroughly soft, according to how much further cooking is planned. Drain, cool, peel and proceed.

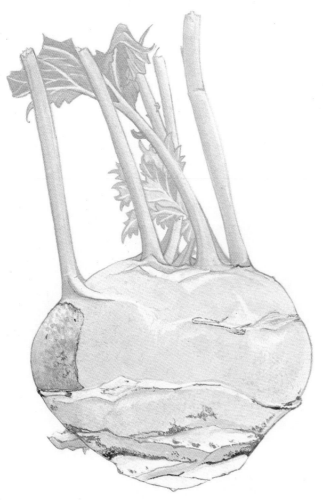

COOKING:

As this vegetable is not widely grown or consumed, East or West, few particular or unique modes of preparing it have been created. Cooks mostly treat it like its cousins, cabbage, cauliflower and radish.

Western. To serve raw, slice in sticks, then nibble, dip or toss in salads. To serve cooked, parboil until almost tender, then slice and sauté, cream, bake au gratin or au fromage. Alternatively, boil until soft, purée for soup, and flavour with dill or caraway and sweet or sour cream.

Chinese. Like the Chinese radish, kohlrabi may be braised or stewed with meat. Like bamboo shoots, it may be included in mixed vegetable dishes for contrast in colour and texture. The Cantonese most commonly serve it with beef, either stir-fried with tender cuts, or parboiled and served plain under a highly flavoured meat sauce. The recipes described for Oriental radish (p. 90) go equally well with kohlrabi. Or try the following:

Oyster Beef & Kohlrabi

Kohlrabi
Tender beef, shredded and seasoned
Oyster sauce, approximately 2–3 tablespoons per cup beef
Clove(s) of garlic, crushed
White wine

Parboil whole kohlrabi as described above; then peel and chop in large matchsticks.

Heat oil in wok; add garlic, when fragrant remove and add beef. Stir and toss until almost cooked. Add oyster sauce, a good dash of wine, and any liquid which has accumulated under the kohlrabi. Stir to blend flavours; quickly adjust seasoning and thickness of sauce. Either return kohlrabi and toss together with the beef, or simply pour sauce over kohlrabi on serving dish and serve.

YAM BEAN OR JICAMA
Saa got 沙葛

APPEARANCE: This is the only vegetable with a narrow neck and lobed bottom. It varies from 5″ to 8″ in length, and its skin has a sandy colour and texture.

QUALITY: Select sound, solid, wormless vegetables. Smaller, younger ones are more tender.

GENERAL COMMENTS: The English name of this vegetable derives from the fact that the mother plant produces both bean-like pods and yam-like tubers. The pods are poisonous, but the flesh of the tubers (as illustrated) is white, crunchy, sweet, sometimes slightly fibrous, and edible raw or cooked. The Mexican name, jicama, reflects the fact that the vegetable's native home is tropical America, although it has been cultivated in Southeast Asia since the Spaniards introduced it to the Philippines in the seventeenth century.

PREPARATION: Peel off the thin, sand-coloured outer skin together with the layer of white fibrous flesh just beneath it. Slice as desired.

COOKING:
Western. Eat raw: nibble sticks; toss slivers in salads; dip slices. For Mexican hors d'oeuvres, serve slices with guacamole (mashed avocado) dip or, more traditionally, with wedges of fresh lime and chilli pepper-salt dip.
   To cook jicama, treat it like potatoes: cream, steam, braise, boil, bake or mash.
Chinese. In Cantonese style, simply stir-fry slices of jicama with beef, pork or shrimp, either plain or with black beans and garlic. Alternatively, serve it beneath a sauce of beef and onions, or oyster beef as described for kohlrabi, or a slightly sour sauce of squid and haam suen choi, as described on p. 23.
   In restaurant style, substitute rectangular slices of jicama for bamboo shoots in any medley of meat and vegetables as a source of contrasting crispness and light sweetness.

WATER CHESTNUTS
Ling gok 菱角

APPEARANCE: The bizarre shape of these nuts leaves no room for misidentification. They measure about 2″ from tip to tip, with a smooth shell as hard as the horns they resemble. The inner nutmeat, sometimes sold shelled, is also wing-tipped but creamy-white in colour, as illustrated.

QUALITY: Unshelled nuts are difficult to evaluate. Choose those which look sound and smell fresh. When cracked, the meat should fill the inner cavity and be uniformly white in colour.

GENERAL COMMENTS: Three species of the genus *Trapa* have been providing human food since neolithic times. *T. bicornuta*, the true water chestnut and the species illustrated here, was one of the five most important grains used in China before the 20th century; *T. bispinosa*, the Singhara nut, also with two horns, is eaten by the people of Kashmir; while *T. natans*, the Jesuit's nut, with four horns, seems to have been a common food of most ancient Europeans.

"Ling gok" resemble potatoes in three respects. First, they are white and starchily sweet but otherwise bland in flavour. Second, they have a crunchy texture when raw and a somewhat mealy texture when cooked. Third, they must be eaten well cooked. The Chinese water chestnut (p. 100) has surpassed the true water chestnut in popularity because it is sweeter, easier to grow, and edible either raw or cooked.

Water chestnuts in the shell will keep refrigerated several weeks. Shelled nuts must be eaten within two days of purchase because they very quickly decay. Check each nutmeat carefully for soft spots before using.

PREPARATION: Remove outer shell with a nutcracker.

COOKING:

Western. Treat these like tiny new potatoes: boil, then toss in butter, with minced spring onions, shallots, herbs or bits of bacon.

Chinese. For most Cantonese, water chestnuts are a delicacy to be eaten during the Mid-Autumn Moon Festival. For Chiu Chow Chinese, they are a hearty vegetable to be eaten throughout the year, either braised with pork like taro (p. 89) or boiled in soup.

CHINESE CHESTNUTS
Lut tzee 栗子

APPEARANCE: Appropriate for their northern origins, these nuts have two coats: an outer, hard, smooth shell; and an inner, furry, beige membrane which closely covers the convoluted yellow nutmeat. In markets, vendors may have nuts in any or all of the stages: some unshelled, fully clothed; some in just their underwear; and some naked.

QUALITY: Select firm, unblemished nuts, with no signs of rot, worms or bruises. The inner nut should be uniformly yellow and solid. The safest course is to buy peeled nuts, although you will pay extra both for the convenience of having them ready-to-eat and for the assurance that they are sound.

GENERAL COMMENTS: Although edible raw, these nuts are usually cooked, either roasted, baked, boiled or braised. Their taste is sweet and rich, their texture a bit pasty or mealy.

Chestnuts are a northern temperate crop, familiar to Asians, Europeans and Americans. All trees belong to the same genus, but each continent seems to have its own species. Thus appearances, tastes and textures differ, but only slightly.

Unpeeled nuts should remain fresh for at least a month if stored in a dry plastic bag in the refrigerator.

PREPARATION: For roasting or baking, leave unshelled. For boiling or braising, remove outer shell with a nutcracker and, in some fashion, remove the furry inner skin. Regardless of the method this is tedious. Some cooks recommend parboiling the nuts and peeling them while warm; others prefer to simply scrape and peel the raw nuts with a knife.

COOKING:

Western. In the West, chestnuts are a winter delicacy traditionally associated with Christmas. In England chestnut purée is indispensable for stuffing the Christmas goose, while in France chestnuts are served either as "marrons glacées" preserved in sugar, or as purée in mousses and other desserts.

In a nutshell, then, roast or boil whole chestnuts and eat out of hand. Or shell, boil until soft, mash, and use with savoury ingredients to stuff poultry or fowl, or with sweet rich ingredients to make desserts.

Chinese. Most chestnuts imported into Hong Kong are consumed from small bags purchased from street vendors who roast them in mounds of charcoal. At home, cooks may braise them with chicken, serve them in sauce over Peking cabbage, or boil them in sweet soup.

Lut Tzee Munn Gai

Chicken pieces
Chinese chestnuts, shelled and peeled
Garlic, crushed
Light and dark soy sauces

In a braising pot, fry garlic in a little oil until fragrant. Add chicken to brown lightly. Add chestnuts with approximately equal amounts light and dark soy sauces, a bit of sugar and water to about one-half the depth of the ingredients. Simmer until chestnuts are tender and liquid is reduced, about $1-1\frac{1}{2}$ hours. Periodically check, stir and add more water if the casserole has cooked dry. When ready to serve, remove chicken to serving dish, adjust seasoning of sauce, thicken it with cornstarch, and pour over chicken.

Wann Ding Bo

12 Chinese chestnuts, shelled and peeled
$\frac{1}{2}$ cup barley (yee mai 薏米)
1 sheet dried bean curd skin (foo jook 腐竹), cut in strips
6 quail eggs (aam chunn daan 鵪鶉蛋) or 3 hen's eggs, hard-boiled and shelled
Sugar to taste

Combine chestnuts, barley and bean curd skin with 6 cups of water. Bring to a boil and simmer until chestnuts are tender and barley has swollen. Sweeten to taste. Add eggs and, when heated through, serve.

CHINESE WATER CHESTNUTS
Ma taai 馬蹄

APPEARANCE: These mahogany-coloured balls are usually 1–2″ in diameter, encircled with triangular leaf scales and encrusted with dirt.

QUALITY: Firm, unbruised, unsprouted nuts are best, although the mud and dark skin often prevent accurate discrimination of the bad from the good.

GENERAL COMMENTS: Ma taai have a crunchy, succulent texture and sweetly nutty taste. They may be eaten raw or cooked. Once you have acquired some fresh ma taai, however, eat them within a week. Due to their high water and sugar content, bruises and bad spots soon ferment and quickly send off-flavours through the whole nut.

For accuracy's sake please note that there are, in fact, two very different beasts which go by the name "water chestnut." The true water chestnut, known to the Cantonese as "ling gok," is a horn-shaped nut (see p. 97), while the Chinese water chestnut described and illustrated here is a root-like organ (or corm, to the botanists). It is these ma taai which are canned and which are the source of water chestnut flour.

Canned water chestnuts are an acceptable substitute for fresh, and are edible straight from the can.

PREPARATION: Wash; peel. This is a tedious task. The flesh should be pure white, crisp, cleanly sweet; discard any which are not.

To store peeled nuts put them in a jar and cover with slightly salted or sugared water. Some of the chestnuts' flavour will leach into the water, but that is the price for the convenience of peeling them all at once.

COOKING:

Western. Eat out of hand as a snack or dessert. Combine in fruit, lettuce or vegetable salads, particularly with other nuts. Wrap in bacon, grill and serve as hors d'oeuvres.

Chinese. The Cantonese associate water chestnuts with sweets, tonic soups and savoury minced meat dishes but not with stir-fried vegetables.

(N.B. This is not to say that water chestnuts cannot be or should not be or do not taste good when stir-fried; only that the method is unknown among the 5 million Chinese people in Hong Kong.)

The easiest, if not the most common, way the Cantonese consume ma taai is simply freshly peeled, as a snack. Traditional housewives use them to boil tonic soups, usually with the more esoteric parts of pigs, such as spleen, stomach and intestines. Or they use them to prepare "Ma Taai Go." Exactly like the savoury "Loh Baak Go," this sweet version

is mixed, steamed until solid, sliced in squares and fried lightly to serve. In homes it is most commonly prepared at Chinese New Year, while in Cantonese restaurants it is served year-round as a dim sum at lunchtime.

Yet another way to serve these crunchy morsels is in minced meat mixtures. Grate them, and mix with minced beef and onions as a filling for deep-fried wonton, or with minced pork and preserved cabbage as in the following Cantonese classic:

Mooi Choi Jing Yuk Bang

Chinese preserved cabbage, mooi choi (梅菜)
Chinese water chestnuts, peeled, grated
Lean pork meat, minced
(Winter mushrooms, soaked, chopped finely)
(Chilli peppers, minced)

Use approximately equal parts of all ingredients, with just a touch of chilli to taste. Rinse mooi choi well to remove excess salt; squeeze relatively dry and chop finely. Combine all ingredients and season with a dash of light soy sauce and a little cornstarch. Pat into a shallow dish or enamel pan, dribble with cooked oil. Steam over water or cooking rice until pork is cooked.

Alternatively, the mixture may be stir-fried or shaped into patties and browned like hamburgers.

SWEET POTATO
Faan sue 蕃薯

APPEARANCE: Literally hundreds of varieties of sweet potatoes are grown throughout the world, so tubers can vary dramatically in size, shape and colour as well as taste and texture. The skin can be white, yellow, orange, purple or brown in colour (although generally shades of orange predominate), and likewise the flesh. Sweet potatoes resemble ordinary white potatoes in size and smoothness of skin, but differ in shape. Note the distinct taper at both ends of these tubers.

QUALITY: Tubers with yellow flesh are sweeter, finer-grained and more nutritious (more carotene, the precursor of Vitamin A) than white-fleshed types. These potatoes do not keep well, especially if they have not been cured properly, so check carefully for signs of rot.

GENERAL COMMENTS: Cooked sweet potatoes are starchy, soft and sweet, with a taste not unlike baked winter squash or roasted chestnuts in certain varieties.

Botanically, of course, sweet potatoes are not potatoes at all, nor are they yams, although all three can be cooked in much the same ways. Sweet potato is the oldest cultivated tuber of the trio, and it continues to be the most widely cultivated root crop in Southeast Asia.

PREPARATION: Wash; leave intact (i.e. in skin) for baking; or peel and chop as desired.

COOKING:

Western. Like white potatoes, these may be sliced thinly and deep-fried, boiled or baked in their jackets. Once cooked, the flesh may be puréed, mashed or sieved, seasoned and served as a savoury vegetable or sweet dessert. For the former, beat in salt, pepper and sweet or sour cream. For the latter, add sugar or honey to taste, chopped nuts and spices such as cinnamon, nutmeg and ginger.

Chinese. In Hong Kong sweet potatoes are most often served sweet:

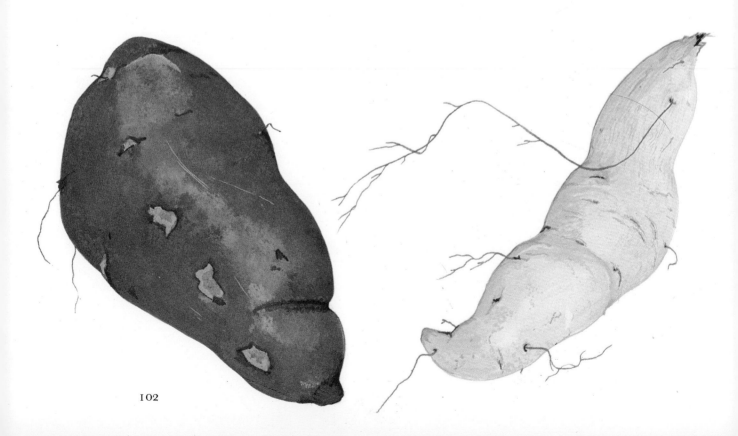

Faan Sue Soup

Wash tubers well, peel, chop coarsely. Add water: 2–4 cups per large tuber. Bring to a boil and simmer gently until tubers are quite soft and broth is well flavoured. Sweeten with sugar, using either Chinese slab sugar (peen tong 片糖) or brown sugar, to taste; serve hot.

Add a piece of ginger or a stick of cinnamon as the soup boils if you think spice is nice.

Deep-fried Sweet Potato Balls

Sweet potato
Peanut butter
Sesame seeds
Wheat or rice flour

Boil sweet potatoes until soft. Mash flesh, season with white sugar. Add enough flour to make a stiff dough. Pinch off a bit of dough; form into a flat circle, place a dab of peanut butter in the centre, pull edges up and seal into a small ball. Roll in sesame seeds; deep-fry until golden.

PAPAYA
Muk gwa 木瓜

APPEARANCE: Broadly grooved bullet shape and smooth skin of green-turning-orange colour distinguish this fruit. Inside, the flesh is red to orange in colour, with a central cavity occupied by black beady seeds. Of the many varieties grown, some have a narrow shape, 15″ long and 4–5″ in diameter, while others have a shape which is almost spherical, 5–8″ in diameter, as illustrated.

QUALITY: The best quality for cooking is slightly under-ripe, signified by a predominantly green colour. Ripe papayas are sweet to eat but too soft to cook.

GENERAL COMMENTS: Papaya originated in southern Mexico, reached the Philippines during the 16th century, and took another hundred years to spread through the tropics and subtropics, including southeast China, where it is now widely grown in home gardens.

Ripe fruits are sweet enough to class as dessert, while unripe ones, only mildly sweet, have a texture firm enough to cook. The flesh is as smooth as avocado ice cream.

PREPARATION: Slice lengthwise in half; remove seeds. For cooking, peel.

COOKING:

Western. Serve ripe and raw, sliced in wedges, as a table fruit. A squeeze of lemon or lime and a pinch of salt add a delightful accent.

Chinese. Cantonese use fruit grown locally when two-thirds ripe to prepare both sweet and savoury soups.

Savoury Papaya Soup

Papaya, peeled and chopped
1 slice of fresh ginger, crushed
Either: Lean pork meat, shredded;
       Tail of a grass carp; or
       Pork ribs

If using fish, scale, rinse, dry, rub with salt, then fry lightly until golden on both sides. Combine fish or meat, ginger and papaya in a pot of water. Bring to the boil, simmer at least one hour, season with salt and pepper, and serve.

Double-boiled Sweet Papaya Soup

1 papaya, peeled, chopped in large chunks
$\frac{1}{2}$–1 cup Chinese rock sugar (bing tong 冰糖); or white or brown sugar

Place ingredients in double boiler over simmering water; cook 1–2 hours. The papaya will gradually generate its own broth. When the chunks have softened to the point of disintegration, serve the soup.

Chinese home-style double boilers are fashioned by placing a heatproof pot or casserole on top of a dish or trivet inside a larger pot of boiling water. The lid of the inner pot must extend beyond the rim of the pot itself to prevent water from leaking inside. The boiling water should reach about halfway up the side of the inner pot and must be replenished periodically.

This elaborate process is not strictly necessary—the soup can be simply boiled in water—but it is worthwhile because double-boiling preserves delicate flavours otherwise driven off by high temperature.

KUDZU
Fun got 粉葛

APPEARANCE: A combination of characters distinguishes this root from others. First, it is unusually large: commonly 10–15″ but possibly greater than 2′ in length, and heavy. Its skin is the colour of potatoes but rough in texture; it is bulbous like yam bean but more irregular, elongated and tapered at both ends. A cross-sectional slice will reveal that the flesh is white with concentric rings running parallel to the surface.

QUALITY: Apply criteria as for other roots, selecting firm, wormless individuals.

GENERAL COMMENTS: The flesh of kudzu, like its cousin jicama, is white and sweet but, unlike the latter, it is more than 25% starch and is chew-defyingly tough. Consequently most of the kudzu crop is processed to produce starch which is used in cooking as a thickener for sauces and soups.

    The name "kudzu" is Japanese, although the plant itself is native to the Asian continent. It was cultivated as a staple food throughout Southeast Asia for centuries until more tender, tasty and nutritious crops (like sweet potatoes) were introduced. Nevertheless, kudzu and related species are still being grown extensively throughout the world, not for human food, but as cover crops to prevent erosion, improve the soil and provide fodder for cattle.

PREPARATION: Slice, using a sharp, thin knife and a lot of strength. Peel. Chop coarsely.

COOKING:

To eat fresh kudzu, the Cantonese recommend making soup: Boil with pork, beef or chicken bones for at least two hours. The resulting broth will be remarkably sweet, and the kudzu itself may be edible (if not too old and fibrous).

APPENDIX

The botanical names and historical information recorded here was gleaned primarily from *Vegetables in South-east Asia* by G. A. C. Herklots (1972), and *Tropical Crops: Monocotyledons* and *Tropical Crops: Dicotyledons* by J. W. Purseglove (1975).

PLANTS		VEGETABLES		
	BOTANICAL NAMES	ENGLISH NAMES	CANTONESE PRONUNCIATION	CHINESE CHARACTERS	PAGE

	BOTANICAL NAMES	ENGLISH NAMES	CANTONESE PRONUNCIATION	CHINESE CHARACTERS	PAGE
FUNGI					
	Agaricus campestris	Button or field mushrooms	Yeung kwan	洋菌	—
	Auricularia spp.	Jew's ear mushrooms	Wan yee	云耳	5
	Lentinus edodes	Winter mushrooms	Dong gwoo	冬菇	4
	Volvaria esculenta	Straw mushrooms	Tso gwoo	草菇	80
FLOWERING PLANTS: MONOCOTS					
Alismaceae					
	Sagittaria sinensis Sims	Arrowhead tubers	Tsee goo	慈菇	93
Alliaceae (Onion Family)					
	Allium ampeloprasum L. var. *porrum* (L.) Gay	Leek	Daai suen	大蒜	72
	A. cepa L. var. *aggregatum* G. Don.	Spring onions	Ts'ung	葱	10
	A. cepa L. var. *aggregatum* G. Don.	Shallots	Ts'ung tau	葱頭	11
	A. cepa L. var. *cepa*	Onion	Yeung ts'ung	洋葱	—
	A. sativum L.	Garlic	Suen tau	蒜頭	7
	A. tuberosum Rottl. ex Spreng.	Chinese chives	Gau choi	韮菜	31
	A. tuberosum Rottl. ex Spreng.	Blanched Chinese chives	Gau wong	韮黃	30
	A. tuberosum Rottl. ex Spreng.	Flowering Chinese chives	Gau choi fa	韮菜花	29
Araceae					
	Colocasia esculenta (D.) Schott	Taro	Woo tau	芋頭	88
Cyperaceae (Sedge Family)					
	Eleocharis dulcis (Bur.) Trin. ex Hens.	Chinese water chestnuts	Ma taai	馬蹄	100
Gramineae (Grass Family)					
	Dendrocalamus spp.; *Phyllostachys* spp.	Bamboo shoots	Chuk sun	竹筍	78
	Oryza sativa L.	Rice	Mai	米	1
	Triticum spp.	Wheat	—	—	—
	Zizania aquatica L.	Wild rice shoots	Gaau sun	膠筍	84
Zingiberaceae					
	Zingiber officinale Rosc.	Ginger	Geung	薑	8
	Zingiber officinale Rosc.	Stem ginger	Tsee geung	子薑	82

	PLANTS	VEGETABLES		PAGE
BOTANICAL NAMES	ENGLISH NAMES	CANTONESE PRONUNCIATION	CHINESE CHARACTERS	
FLOWERING PLANTS: DICOTS				
Amarantaceae				
Amaranthus gangeticus L.	Chinese spinach	Een choi	莧菜	34
Anacardiaceae				
Dracontome dao (Blanco) Merr. & Rolfe	Dracontomelum	Yun meen	人面	85
Basellaceae				
Basella alba L.	Ceylon spinach	Saan choi	潺菜	36
Brassicaceae (Mustard Family)				
Brassica alboglabra Bailey	Chinese kale	Gaai laan	芥蘭	21
B. chinensis Jus. var. *chinensis*	Chinese white cabbage	Baak choi	白菜	16
B. chinensis Jus. var. *parachinensis* (Bailey) Tsen & Lee	Chinese flowering cabbage	Choi sum	菜心	15
B. chinensis Jus. var. *rosularis* Tsen & Lee	Chinese flat cabbage	Taai goo choi	大古菜	20
B. juncea (L.) Czern. & Coss. var. *rugosa* (Roxb.) Tsen & Lee	Mustard cabbages:			
	Bamboo mustard cabbage	Chuk gaai choi	竹芥菜	24
	Swatow mustard cabbage	Daai gaai choi	大芥菜	22
	(Salted mustard cabbage)	(Haam suen choi)	咸酸菜	23
	Sow cabbage	Jiu la choi	豬婼菜	25
B. oleracea L. var. *botrytis*	Broccoli	Gaai laan fa	芥蘭花	—
B. oleracea L. var. *botrytis*	Cauliflower	Yeh choi fa	椰菜花	26
B. oleracea L. var. *capitata* L.	Head cabbage	Yeh choi	椰菜	26
B. oleracea L. var. *gongylodes* L.	Kohlrabi	Gaai laan tau	芥蘭頭	94
B. pekinensis (Lour.) Rupr.	Peking cabbage	Wong nga baak	黃芽白	18
B. rapa L.	Turnip	Choi tau	菜頭	—
Nasturtium officinale R. Br.	Watercress	Sai yeung choi	西洋菜	28
Raphanus sativus L.	Radish (small red)	Hung loh baak jai	紅蘿蔔仔	—
R. sativus L. var. *longipinnatus* Bailey	Oriental radish	Loh baak	蘿蔔	90
R. sativus L. var. *longipinnatus* Bailey	Green oriental radish	Tseng loh baak	菁蘿蔔	92
Caricaceae				
Carica papaya L.	Papaya	Muk gwa	木瓜	104
Compositae				
Artemisia lactiflora Wall.	White wormwood	Junn jiu choi	珍珠菜	41
Chrysanthemum coronarium L. var. *spatiosum* Bailey	Garland chrysanthemum	Tong ho	茼蒿	42
Lactuca sativa L. var. *asparagina* Bailey	Stem lettuce	Woh sun	萵芛	73

BOTANICAL NAMES	ENGLISH NAMES	CANTONESE PRONUNCIATION	CHINESE CHARACTERS	PAGE
L. sativa L. var. *capitata* L.	Head lettuce	Sai saang choi	西生菜	—
L. sativa L. var. *crispa* L.	Leaf lettuce	Saang choi	生菜	38
L. sativa L. var. *longifolia* Lam.	Cos lettuce			—
Convolvulaceae (Morning Glory Family)				
Ipomoea aquatica Forsk.	Water spinach	Ong choi	甕菜	32
I. batatas (L.) Lam.	Sweet potato	Faan sue	蕃薯	102
Cucurbitaceae (Melon Family)				
Benincasa hispida (Thunb.) Cogn.	Winter melon	Dong gwa	冬瓜	56
B. hispida (Thunb.) Cogn. var.	Fuzzy melon	Tseet gwa	節瓜	58
Cucumis sativus L.	Cucumber	Tseng gwa	青瓜	62
Cucumis sativus L.	Yellow cucumber	Wong gwa	黃瓜	63
Cucurbita moschata (Duch. ex Lam.) Duch. ex Poir.	Winter squash	Naam gwa	南瓜	68
Lagenaria siceraria (Mol.) Standl.	Bottle gourd	Woo lo gwa	葫蘆瓜	60
Lagenaria siceraria (Mol.) Standl.	Hairy gourd	Po gwa	蒲瓜	60
Luffa acutangula (L.) Roxb.	Angled luffa	Sze gwa	絲瓜	65
L. cylindrica (L.) M. J. Roem.	Smooth or sponge luffa	Seui gwa	水瓜	65
Momordica charantia L.	Bitter melon	Foo gwa	苦瓜	66
Sechium edule (Jacq.) Swartz	Chayote	Faat sau gwa	佛手瓜	64
Fagaceae (Oak Family)				
Castanea dentata	Chestnut (North American)			—
C. mollissima	Chinese chestnut	Lut tzee	栗子	98
C. sativa Mill.	Chestnut (European)			—
Leguminosae (Bean Family)				
Glycine max (L.) Merr.	Soybean sprouts	Daai dau nga choi	大豆芽菜	50
Glycine max (L.) Merr.	Bean curd	Dau foo	豆腐	52
Pacchyrhizus erosus (L.) Urban	Jicama	Saa got	沙葛	96
Phaseolus aureus Roxb.	Mungbean sprouts	Sai dau nga choi	細豆芽菜	47
Phaseolus aureus Roxb.	Mungbean vermicelli	Fun see	粉絲	5
P. vulgaris L.	French green beans	Been dau	扁豆	—
Pisum sativum L.	Pea shoots	Dau miu	豆苗	37
P. sativum L. var. *macrocarpon* Ser.	Edible peapods	Hoh laan dau	荷蘭豆	46
Pueraria thunbergiana (Sieb. & Zucc.) Benth.	Kudzu	Fun got	粉葛	106
Vigna sesquipedalis (L.) Fruw.	Long beans	Dau gok	豆角	44

PLANTS

VEGETABLES

BOTANICAL NAMES	ENGLISH NAMES	CANTONESE PRONUNCIATION	CHINESE CHARACTERS	PAGE
Nymphaceae				
Nelumbo nucifera Gaerth	Lotus root	Leen ngau	蓮藕	86
Onagraceae				
Trapa bicornis Osb.	Water chestnuts	Ling gok	菱角	97
Solanaceae				
Lycium chinense Mill.	Chinese box thorn	Gau gei choi	枸杞菜	35
Lycopersicon esculentum Mill.	Tomato	Faan kei	蕃茄	—
Solanum melongena L.	Eggplant	Ai gwa	矮瓜	74
S. tuberosum L.	Potato	Sue jai	薯仔	—
Capsicum annuum L. var. *grossum* Sendt.	Sweet green pepper	Tseng jiu	青椒	70
C. annuum L. var. *minimum* (Mill.) Heiser	Cayenne pepper			
C. frutescens L.	Tabasco pepper			
C. annuum L. (several varieties)	Chilli peppers	Laat jiu	辣椒	14
Umbelliferae				
Apium graveolens L.	Celery	Kunn choi	芹菜	76
Coriandrum sativum L.	Coriander	Uen sai	芫茜	12
Daucus carota L. subsp. *sativus* (Hoffm.) Arc.	Carrot	Hung loh baak	紅蘿蔔	—
Petroselinum crispum (Mill.) Nym.	Parsley	Faan uen sai	蕃芫茜	—

INDEX